Abner A. Kingman

Hawaiian club papers

Abner A. Kingman

Hawaiian club papers

ISBN/EAN: 9783743306103

Manufactured in Europe, USA, Canada, Australia, Japa

Cover: Foto ©Andreas Hilbeck / pixelio.de

Manufactured and distributed by brebook publishing software (www.brebook.com)

Abner A. Kingman

Hawaiian club papers

HAWAIIAN CLUB PAPERS.

EDITED BY A COMMITTEE OF THE CLUB.

OCTOBER, 1868.

BOSTON:
PRESS OF ABNER A. KINGMAN,
1868.

Entered according to Act of Congress, in the year 1868, by
THE HAWAIIAN CLUB,
in the Clerk's Office of the District Court for the District of Massachusetts.

EDITIONS.
FOUR HUNDRED AND FIFTY COPIES PLAIN;
FIFTY CLUB COPIES TINTED.

TABLE OF CONTENTS.

The Hawaiian Club,	E. P. Bond,	1
Early Wells of Honolulu,	James Hunnewell,	2
Voyages of the Ancient Hawaiians (From Kamakau),	S. B. Dole,	4
The Hawaiian Translations of the Scriptures,	E. W. Clark,	7
Kaumualii's Diamond,		01
Anecdote of Kamehameha,		11
Story of Paao (From Kamakau),	S. B. Dole,	13
Production and Consumption of Sugar,		17
Hawaii at the "Exposition Universelle," Paris, 1867,	J. F. Hunnewell,	18
Islands of the North Pacific,		29
First Printing at the Hawaiian Islands,	J. F. Hunnewell,	38
A Missionary Episode,	S. B. Dole,	38
Eruption of the Hawaiian Volcanoes,	W. T. Brigham,	40
The Hawaiian Flora,	W. T. Brigham,	45
Rev. Asa Thurston,		49
J. P. Parker,		50
Current Events,		52
Table of Exports and Imports for 1867,		58
A List of Books published at or relating to the Hawaiian Islands,	W. T. Brigham,	63
The Hawaiian National Hymn,	Mrs. Lilia K. Dominis,	116
Constitution and By-Laws of the Hawaiian Club,		118
List of Officers and Members,		119

HAWAIIAN CLUB PAPERS.

THE HAWAIIAN CLUB.

THE Hawaiian Club was formed in January, 1866, by a few gentlemen, who having, at different periods during the last forty years, resided at the Hawaiian Islands, felt that strong attachment for them which is so general among those who have once lived there. Their object was partly to revive pleasant associations by occasional meetings to discuss the past and present condition of Hawaii, and partly to advance the prosperity of the country and the interests of the United States and her citizens there, by calling attention to the great importance of the group, political and commercial, and by collecting and diffusing information in regard to its past history and present condition.

In furtherance of these objects the Club has met once a month, usually in the city of Boston, but occasionally in a more social way at the country residence of some one of its members.

It has corresponded with the friends of Hawaii, resident at the Islands. It has sought, through delegations at Washington, and through newspaper publications and personal interviews of its officers and members with men of influence, to further every measure which would benefit the Islands, such as the establishment of steam mail communication between San Francisco and Honolulu, and the negotiation and ratification of a treaty of commercial reciprocity between the United States and Hawaiian Governments.

Interesting facts relating to the past and passing history of Hawaii have frequently been called forth at the meetings of the Club. Many of these facts have never been recorded, and it has been proposed that they should be reduced to writing by their narrators, and that such of them as may be deemed of sufficient interest and value should be printed for the use of the members of the Club, and of those who take an especial interest in Hawaiian affairs.

In pursuance of this purpose, the present sheets are published as an experiment; and it has been determined to publish in this form, statistics and other material relating to the Islands which might be useful to members of the Club, and which at present is in a much less accessible form. It is hoped that in this way valuable information may be conveniently preserved.

In an appendix will be found the articles of organization of the Club, and a list of its officers and members.

EARLY WELLS OF HONOLULU.

The first attempt to dig a well at Honolulu was made by Wm. R. Warren, an American, about the year 1820, in the central part of the village as it then was, and in nearly the highest part. He went down through the yellow loam and volcanic sand some eight or nine feet, to the great bed of coral that underlies the whole town. The loam caved in, making a frightfully large hole. The superstitions of the natives were aroused by some foreigners who were hostile to anything American, and that fearful hole had to be abandoned.

The first successful effort to dig a well was made some two years later, by Joseph Navarro, a New Yorker, in his yard, afterwards owned by Stephen Reynolds, not far from the Bethel, if my reckoning is correct (and not far from my old sandal-wood storehouse, not a vestige of which has been seen for upwards of forty years), some three or four hundred feet from the shore. He went down about eighteen feet; eight or ten feet through loam and volcanic sand, and some eight feet through the coral bed, the upper surface of which was very uneven. The bottom of the coral bed was as uneven as the top, and the whole was full of cavities and channels through which the fresh water ran towards the shore.

Through the coral the well was hewn with an ordinary American woodaxe. Near the middle of the bed, a hard, projecting lump was found, which required several blows of the axe to part it from the surrounding mass, and in falling, it drew with it what at first seemed to be a knot several inches long, but on examination proved to be a bone of the size and shape of a human thighbone. I, with others, handled it, and, at the time, was of opinion that it was a human bone, and this opinion was strengthened by the fact that from one of the cavities before mentioned in the coral bed, the skull of a human being was taken, in good order and preservation, but darker than a new skull. It evidently had some strength in it as it was kicked about by boys. The cavities did not communicate with the surface. Neither myself, nor any who saw these remains, were naturalists, and the opportunity of describing and preserving these most interesting fossils was neglected.

The second well was dug in 1822, I think, on a part of the Holmes premises occupied by Captain Wm. H. Davis, nearly opposite the main entrance of the estate now (1868) owned by Charles Brewer, Esq., and I think near the northern line of the present Fort Street. The ground here is a very little higher than where the Navarro well was located, and this second well was three or four hundred yards from the first in a northeasterly direction. The substrata proved to be the same as in the former case, and the coral was full of cavities, from which were taken a number of small bones, which I, with several others, examined and considered the bones of a man's hand or foot.

From the facts related and on reflection, I am led to the conclusion that the Islands were inhabited by man, before and during the formation of that vast body of coral that underlies Honolulu.

Many of the present wells, especially those on the plain east of Honolulu, towards Waikiki, pass through the coral bed, which is full of cavities and cracks, and is permeated with streams of fresh water from the mountains. They are usually sunk nearly to the sea level. In one well on this plain a strong current sets constantly from the mountains to the sea.

VOYAGES OF THE ANCIENT HAWAIIANS.

The ancient melès and legends mention the arrival of canoes at these Islands a very long time ago, probably about the commencement of the Christian Era, and speak of other lands and things which were seen by the men who came in them, in the great ocean.

Formerly the Hawaiians included the island of Bolabola and other foreign countries, under the one name, Kahiki; and thus, at this day, all who sail to foreign lands are called " Poe Holokahiki."

In the history and genealogies of the forefathers of the nation, from Kumuhonua to the time of Welaahilaninui and his wife Owe, there were twenty generations of men. Because of their wanderings they said that they had no home, nor any land that they could call their own, till they landed on the shores of the Hawaiian Islands. This is certain, that they came first from Kahiki, and their descendants after them were acquainted with the route thither, and to other lands.

Papa, who was called Wahinui, and also Haumea by some, (which is incorrect, for Haumea was a different personage, being a Goddess, and her offspring belonged to the family of the Gods,) gave birth to a son who became the progenitor of chiefs and people.

It is said that Papa at last sailed to Nuumehalani, where her father Kukalaniehu, and her mother Kahakauakoko, lived, an island guarded on all sides by lofty precipices, and there Papa still renews her youth; about whom the men of Kalaikuahulu, who are skilled in genealogies and legends, sung:—

> " Return, O Papa, from the islands of Kahiki:
> Jealous anger burns the hearts of Wakea's concubines,
> Deep affection stirs the bosom of thy husband."

The ancients possessed accounts of a large whirlpool which they called Moanawàikaioo, which was often alluded to in their traditions. They had also discovered the Black Sea and the Green Sea and the Red Sea; thus runs the old song:—

> " A sea tossing ships,
> A sea of burning coals,
> Is the azure sea of Kane.

> The birds sip the waters of the Red Sea;
> And the waters of the Green Sea.
> Never silent, never quiet, never sleeping
> Are the gently breaking waters of the rippling sea."

The old Hawaiians often mentioned the land of dwarfs; a land where the people, said they, were so small that one ordinary man could carry ten of them. Punaluu is reported to have brought one of these little men to Kau on Hawaii, and he lived at Moaula, inland from Kopu. Wahanui also brought a pair of "Siamese twins" from some country to Kauai, where they were seen by the Kauaiians.

Many Hawaiians in those times sailed to Nuuhiva, to Bolabola, to Upolu, to Savaii, to Kolaniku, to Holanimoe, to Kakukake, to Lalokapu, to Kuukuu, to Malimali, to Muliwaiolena, to Mookuululu, and to many other places, as we learn by the legends and the prophecies and the prayers for discovering other countries.

Such are the traditions of the settlement of these islands, and of the navigation and discoveries of the Hawaiians, as handed down from the past.

TRADITION OF KAULU.

Kaulu was born at Kailua Koolaupoko, fifteen generations from the time of Welaahilaninui. He said that he had visited every land, and had seen all the kingdoms of the world; that he looked into the Maelstrom Waikaioo, and visited the great continents, which are Asia and Europe. He was the explorer who brought back the edible dirt of Kawainui. In his hymn recounting the success of his voyage around the world, thus he speaks:—

> "I am Kaulu
> The adopted son of Kalona.
> The far-seeing explorer;
> Who forbiddeth sleep;
> Who watcheth for the daybreak,
> Who hurleth the spear.
> Kaulu of the land. Kaulu of the sea.
> O! Kaulu the builder of canoes,
> O! Kaulu the pilot of a fleet.
> Thou spannest the heavens.
> Thou cans't grasp the night and the day;
> Thou cans't reach out to the ends of the earth.
> All lands are explored by Kaulu.

All lands are finished by Kaulu,
Even to the coral reefs where the sea thunders.
From the times, perhaps, of Ku,
From the times, perhaps, of Lono
Greatness has degenerated.
By the witness of these shells, of this fish skin,
By the witness of these necklaces,
Is this flight of Kela proved.
Is this flight to the Northern whirlpool proved.
By my father Kakulani,
By my father's bones, I swear."

Whatever may be the veracity of Kaulu in this, his story, the fact of his voyage to Kahiki, at any rate, is true.

TRADITION OF HEMA.

Hema, who was born at Hana, East Maui, was one of those who went to Kahiki. He lived sixteen generations after Kaulu. Just before the birth of his son Kahai, at Iao Wailuku, he sailed for Kahiki to receive the tax (*palala*) for the birth of his son, for his wife was from Kahiki, as were her parents and grandmother. Hema was not heard from afterwards. When Kahai grew up, he asked of his mother: " Where is my father?" His mother answered: " Your father went to Kahiki to receive the palala for you, but the pilots, perchance, were led astray by the Aianukea, the bird of Kane, for he has never returned." Then said Kahai to his mother: "I will search for my father." Thus speak the prophets of his voyage: —

" The rainbow of the path of Kahai.
Then Kahai arose and stirred himself;
Kahai answered to the bright cloud of Kane;
The eyes of Alihi are troubled;
Kahai looked up at the slanting light
Which shone on men and on canoes,
From above the Southern Star.
This, O Kahai, is the way to look for your father;
Go on over the black waves of the ocean,
Through the thunders of the temple of Heaven.
Then demanded Kane of Kaunloo;
For what is this large fleet
That Kahai is coming in?
I am looking for the path to the South,
There at Kahiki, at Ulupaupau;
To land on the shores of Kahiki."

TRADITION OF PAUMAKAU.

Paumakau was born at Kaneohe Koolaupoka. He went to some foreign land and brought back the foreigners who were white, and called them Kaekae and Malii. A certain prophet told the story in these words : "The strangers were tall, with sparkling eyes, and brought with them rabbits with pink eyes, and large white hogs with red eyes."

These traditions, and others of a similar nature, and the tradition of the sending to Kahiki for chiefs when they were scarce among the Hawaiians, show the wonderful skill of the ancient Hawaiians in navigation. The distance from Hawaii to Kahiki is over three thousand miles, and that these daring men were able to track their way thither and back, without compass, chart, or quadrant, seems wholly incredible, until explained by the light of similar and undeniable facts, which show that the unlettered and barbarous races are often, when occasions demand, blessed with an instinct which, in power and extent, seems little short of direct inspiration.

THE HAWAIIAN TRANSLATIONS OF THE SCRIPTURES.

As the new and revised edition of the Hawaiian Bible has been recently published at New York, Rev. E. W. Clark, who has had the entire charge of stereotyping and printing, was requested to furnish the following account:—

Soon after the Hawaiian language was reduced to writing by the first missionaries, small portions of the Bible were translated and printed. When I joined the Mission in 1828, the Sermon on the Mount, the history of Joseph, and a few pages of the Gospel of Luke had been printed, or were in press. From this time the translation of the Bible became a prominent part of missionary labor, and was urged forward as fast as a knowledge of the language and other circumstances would permit.

The following persons took part, more or less, in the first translation:—

Rev. H. Bingham, Rev. A. Thurston, Rev. Wm. Richards, Rev. A. Bishop, Rev. L. Andrews, Rev. J. S. Green, Rev. E. W. Clark, and Rev. S. Dibble.[1]

The work devolved mainly on the first four above named, as

---

[1] From Dibble's History, the following extract shows more particularly the individual work of the Translators:—

	TRANSLATED BY	FIRST PRINTED IN	
Genesis,	Thurston and Bishop,	Honolulu,	1836.*
Exodus,	Richards,	"	" *
Leviticus,	Bingham,	"	" *
Numbers,	Thurston and Bishop,	"	" *
Deuteronomy,	" "	"	" *
Joshua,	Richards,	"	" *
Judges and Ruth,	"	"	1835.
I. Samuel,	Thurston,	"	"
II. Samuel,	Bishop,	"	"
I. Kings,	Bingham and Clark,	"	1838.
II. Kings,	Thurston,	"	"
I. Chronicles,	Bishop,	"	"
II. Chronicles,	Green,	Lahaina,	1836.
Ezra,	Thurston,	Honolulu,	1839.
Nehemiah,	Dibble,	Lahaina,	1835.
Esther,	Richards,	"	"
Job,	Thurston,	Honolulu,	1839.
Psalms, 1-75,	Bingham,	"	(1831-9.)
Psalms, 76-150,	Richards,	"	"
Proverbs,	Andrews,	Lahaina,	1836.
Ecclesiastes,	Green,	"	"
Solomon's Song,	"	"	"
Isaiah, Jeremiah,	Richards,	"	1836-8.
Lamentations,	"	"	"
Ezekiel,	Bingham,	Honolulu,	1839.
Daniel,	Green,	"	"
Hosea, Habakkuk,	Thurston,	"	"
Zephaniah, Malachi,	Bishop,	"	"
Matthew,	Bingham and Thurston,	Rochester, N. Y.,	1828.*
Mark,	Richards,	"	" *
Luke,	Bingham,	Honolulu,	1829.
John,	Thurston,	Rochester,	1828.
Acts,	Richards,	Honolulu,	1829.
Romans,	Thurston and Bishop,	"	1831.
I. Corinthians,	Richards,	"	"
II. Corinthians,	Thurston,	"	"
Galatians,	Thurston and Bishop,	"	"
Philippians,	" "	"	"
Colossians,	Bingham,	"	1832.
Hebrews,	"	"	"
James,	Richards and Andrews,	"	"
I. and II. Peter,	Richards,	"	"
I., II. and III. John,	Richards and Andrews,	"	"
Jude,	" "	?	"
Revelations,	"	?	?

* Selections from the books marked * were published earlier in the form of tracts.—*Dibble, p. 435.*

they had been longer on the ground, and were more familiar with the language. Portions of Scripture when translated by one of the above, passed into the hands of others for revision, before being printed. The Hebrew and Greek texts were consulted, both by the translators and reviewers. Such other helps were employed as could be obtained, especially the help of the most intelligent natives. Separate portions were printed as soon as ready for the press.

The first uniform edition of the New Testament was printed in 1836, and the first edition of the whole Bible in 1839. This was a 12mo, and usually bound in three volumes. An octavo edition of the whole Bible was printed at the Mission Press in 1843. These two editions contained about 20,000 copies in all. Several editions of the New Testament were printed separately, usually numbering about 10,000 to an edition. The expense of these works was borne mainly by the American Bible Society.

While on a visit to this country in 1856, I was requested by the Mission to superintend the electrotyping of a Biglot New Testament, Hawaiian and English, with references. Plates of this work were prepared, and two or three editions have been printed off, and transmitted to the Islands.

In 1857, the Mission, assembled in General Meeting, resolved to make preparations for a new and revised edition of the whole Bible, with marginal references. A committee was appointed to commence the work of revision. The work finally devolved mainly on myself, as chairman of this committee, assisted by Revs. W. P. Alexander, J. F. Pogue, D. Baldwin, Pres. W. D. Alexander, and Rev. A. O. Forbes. In 1864 the revision had so far progressed, that it was decided that I should come to this country to superintend the electrotyping of the work, read proofs, &c., at the Bible House, New York, the Bible Society having kindly offered to prepare plates of the work. The work was commenced at the Bible House in October, 1864, and the plates were completed in the summer of 1867. One edition, in octavo form, and one smaller edition in quarto, have been printed off, with one thousand extra copies of the New Testament. These have been handsomely bound in different styles, and a part of the copies are now on their way to the Islands. A Bible of the quarto form has been elegantly bound, and forwarded to the king, as a present from the American Bible Society.

Plates of a small New Testament, 18mo, more especially for the use of Sabbath and other schools, are now being prepared at the Bible House, under my supervision. When these are completed, we shall have three sets of plates at the Bible House,—one set of the Biglot New Testament, one of the whole Bible, and one of the small Testament. From these, copies can be multiplied as they shall be needed. These plates will probably last as long as the Hawaiian people shall last as a people speaking the Hawaiian language.

New Testament,	12mo,	1836.
" "	8vo,	1837.
" "	"	1843.
" "	8vo, Hawaiian and English,	1857.
" "	18mo,	1868.
Bible,	12mo, 3 vols.	1839.
"	8vo and 4to, pp. 1452,	1843.
"	8vo and 4to, References,	1867.

KAUMUALII'S DIAMOND.

In the early days, after the discovery of the Hawaiian Islands. the chiefs often ordered goods from Europe and the United States, through the shipmasters who traded between those places and the Islands.

On one occasion, during the reign of Kaumualii, King of Kauai, Captain Wiles, who was about to sail for the States, called on him at his royal residence at Waimea, to receive his orders. The captain and his supercargo were ushered into one of the apartments of the grass palace, and after respectfully saluting the king, who reclined *en dishabille* on his *hikie*, seated themselves at a small table, which stood against the side of the room, and prepared to take down the items on paper. Kaumualii, who had been taking his afternoon nap, and was attended only by his *Iwikuamoo*,[1] immediately arose, and wrapping a light *kapa* around his form,

---

[1] Back-scratcher.

seated himself on a brilliant Niihau mat in the coolest part of the room, and after sending out his attendant to order a repast of fish and fowl for his guests, proceeded to business. As he had doubtless already made up his mind as to the articles he wished to order, the list was quickly told off and written down, showing by its contents the character of the man and the circumstances of his little kingdom, as well perhaps as the message of a president or the speech of a premier usually exhibits the condition of a nation. Besides a large assortment of dry goods and hardware, articles of adornment and implements of peace, there was a large order for powder and muskets, and a battery of field-pieces for the benefit of that insolent Kamehameha, who was even then threatening to invade his dominions.

"Is there anything more?" asked the captain, after the chief had finished his enumeration.

The latter, without any reply, arose and paced the floor in silence for about ten minutes, evidently in deep thought; then facing the captain, he answered:—

"I am told that the white kings always have precious stones and diamonds, to add to their glory; now there is only one thing more that I want you to bring me, and that is a diamond."

"How large a diamond shall I get for you?" asked the captain.

"Well, I don't know exactly; how large do they have them?"

The captain never having traded in diamonds, could give no very definite information as to the size of the articles; neither could his supercargo, who, however, ventured the remark that he believed they were not very large. At length, after further unsatisfactory discussion, Kaumualii, with a lordly grunt of relief, settled the question by telling the captain that a diamond of the size of a cocoanut would answer.

History drops its curtain over the result of the negotiation.

ANECDOTE OF KAMEHAMEHA.

IN the last years of his life, Kamehameha the First became a strict temperance man, indulging only at times in light wines.

He also carried his principles into the administration of government, and issued a royal proclamation forbidding the manufacture of distilled or fermented liquors; the penalty for disobedience to this law was the *hao*,[1] a species of confiscation or attainder, in which the wrongdoer was stripped of all his property down even to his calabashes and *malo*, and sometimes banished for a fixed time from the district in which the offence was committed.

Shortly before the death of the king, when he was lying in his palace quite feeble with age and infirmity, his courtiers, thinking that nothing would benefit him so much as stimulants of some kind, which, however, they could not persuade him to take, devised a plan which gave great promise of success. Accordingly, Don Paulo Manini prepared with his usual skill a drink of gin and eggs and sugar and spices, taking care to add liberally the latter constituent, in order to drown the odor of the gin; and then taking the fragrant mixture, he went in unto the king on his hands and knees, and gave it to him to drink. Kamehameha raised himself up on his *hikie*, and took the bowl in both hands and slowly raised it to his lips, but before he had time to taste the contents, his experienced nose detected the flavor of the gin through the disguise of the spicy incense that ascended and filled the room with its tempting aroma, and turning his eyes, terrible in anger, on Don Paulo, who humbly knelt at his feet, without saying a word threw the steaming contents of the bowl into the face of the latter. Paulo Manini, with his eyes painfully smarting, dared not show a sign of anger, or even to wipe his face, but remained motionless, blinking and trembling lest the wrath of Kamehameha, unappeased with this punishment, should lead him to cut him down with his sword, which always lay within his reach, till at last the king gave him a sign of dismission, and he abjectly crawled out of the room; when he was safe outside, his manner of humility changed to one of pride and anger, and as he wiped the remains of the highly spiced egg-nog from his face, he said to his friend who had been waiting the result: "If he do such a thing to me again, —— me, if I no resent it."

It is believed that Manini never gave the water-drinking monarch an opportunity to repeat the offence.

---

[1] All the high chiefs had the power of inflicting the *hao* for all offences not capital; and this practice continued until the people had a written code of laws.

STORY OF PAAO.

MANY centuries after the Hawaiian Islands were settled by the ancestors of the present race of natives, there lived on the island of Upolu a powerful priest, by the name of Paao, who, with his followers, besides their possessions on Upolu, held lands at Vavau, and also at what is now called New Zealand; for they often made long voyages to distant countries.

Now Paao had a brother by the name of Lonopele, who also was a priest, a man of great influence, and skilled in all the arts of divination. And the two brothers cultivated the ground. The land of Lonopele was near the sea, where, with his men, he planted trees, and raised fruit of every kind; and the fruit of his trees was finer than that of any other place. And it came to pass one morning, as Lonopele walked out early among his trees, that he found them stripped of all the ripe fruit; and because he had before seen the son of Paao near the trees, and looking wistfully at them, he suspected that he was the one who had taken the fruit. Therefore he put on his *kihei* and went and found Paao, and told him of his loss, and accused his child of the theft. Paao said to him:

"Surely! thou knowest, perhaps, that thy fruit was taken from the trees by my son?" Lonopele answered:

"I saw the child go there, but indeed did not see him take anything; still I am very certain that he did the mischief."

Then Paao said: "If this be so, I will cut open the stomach of my child, and if I do not find the fruit, what then?"

Then was Lonopele greatly shocked, and he replied:

"This thing is not from me; it is thy proposal alone; when didst thou ever hear of any one cutting open a man to see what was inside of him? Thou alone art responsible."

"It cannot be helped," replied Paao. "I will cut open my son, and if I find the fruit, why then thou are right; but if I do not find any, then thou art wrong."

So Paao, having made up his mind, carried out his purpose, and did not find any fruit. Then he told Lonopele to look for himself; but Lonopele spoke and said:

"Thou alone art the man who examines the insides of a child." And he would not look.

Then Paao mourned with great lamentation for his son. And he said: "I will seek means for the death of thy child, and thus avenge this false accusation. And then I will forsake this land."

Immediately after these things happened, Paao commenced to build and fit out canoes for his voyage. And not many days after, when the canoes were finished, he put the *kapu* upon them, that no man might touch them till the *lolo*[1] had been offered up to the gods for the safety of the canoes. A long time they waited on account of the *kapu*, doing nothing but eating and sleeping. One day the little child of Lonopele wandered down to where the canoes were lying, and amused himself by drumming on them. Paao, hearing the noise, said to his men:

"What is this rumbling sound from the canoes?"

And they said: "The son of Lonopele is drumming on the canoes."

Then he ordered them to catch him and kill him; and they killed him. Then Paao made an end of the *kapu* of the sacrifice; and he took the dead body of the child and laid it on the block on which the hinder part of one of the canoes rested. After two or three days had passed, Lonopele came to some of the men who were at work loading the canoes, in search of his son, greatly troubled lest he was utterly lost. While there, he was much struck by the beauty and perfection of the canoes, for they were very large and well finished. And examining one in particular, as he moved towards the hinder end, he observed a swarm of flies buzzing about under the canoe, and looking more carefully he saw the dead body and recognized it as his own child, and saw that he had been murdered. At this sight he did not hold in his sorrow, but mourned, chanting of his affection for his child, and of his wrath against Paao, in these words: "*Wonderful* art thou, O Paao! thou art the man who, having killed thine own son, have sought occasion against my son, and lo! here thou hast killed him, also; therefore rise up and depart from this land, for thou art a totally bad man." And then Lonopele took his child away with mourning songs of love for him.

At this sentence of banishment against Paao, he made ready all of his supplies for the voyage.

---

[1] The sacrifice (a hog), which, according to custom, was offered up at the completion of canoes.

The number of those who sailed in these canoes, was thirty-eight. There were two stewards to divide out the food; and of the chiefs there was Pili, and his wife Hinaauaku, and Na Mauuowalaia, Paao's sister, who was so named from the grass that Paao brought, from the mountains of Malaia, with him to Hawaii.

Then Paao annointed himself for his voyage of discovery.

And when they all had gone on board of the canoes, and were about to put off, a prophet came and stood on the top of the cliff of Kaakoheo which overhung the beach, and called out to Paao, and said:

"O Paao! let me also be one of those who sail with you."

Paao said, "Who art thou?"

He answered, "A prophet."

"What is thy name?"

"Lelekoae," replied the man.

Then Paao called to him to fly down. So he sprung from the precipice, but was killed in trying to light on the hard ground below. Then many other prophets came to the top of the cliffs, wanting to sail with Paao; but he giving them one by one an opportunity to try their power of flying in like manner, according to the practice of the prophets, they all perished in the attempt.

Then the fleet sailed; and those who waited to see them off went back to their homes, where they met Makuakaumana, and said to him:

"Paao has sailed, and with him the chief Pilikaaiea."

He answered: "I am one who was to have sailed with him."

The men replied: "They have gone off straight out to sea; thou canst not reach them."

Then Makuakaumana ran quickly and stood up on the top of Kaakoheo. And he looked in the direction they had gone, and the canoes were like specks, and only the sails could be seen above the sea.

Then he shouted with a very great shout: "O Paao! I too." Two, or perhaps three times he shouted; and Paao heard the far distant sound faintly, like the echo of a whisper; and he bent his head and listened, and it was as if the sobbing of spirits rose on the air. Then he called out, "Who art thou?"

"A prophet."

"What is thy name?"

"Makuakaumana."

Paao said: "The canoe is full, but there is room for one more on the *momoa*."

"That place is mine," cried the prophet.

Then Paao told him to fly along.

And he flew from the cliff, and over the sea, and came down on the *momoa* of the canoe; and the men of the canoe stretched out their hands to help him. His flying was like the flying of a bird.

Then he spake and said: "Here am I. Where art thou?"

"On the *pola*,"[1] answered Paao.

Thus sung the wise men of Kalaikuahulu of the deeds of Makuakaumana:—

> "Thou art the many pronged flying fish,
> Compassed on all sides by the circle of the sky;
> Going out over the dark waters of the ocean,
> Among the thunders of the home of Kane,
> The creator of the heavens.
> Makuakaumana, the great astrologer,
> Thou hast known the islands,
> Thou hast encircled the horizon of Tahiti,
> Soaring over the sea, thou didst light on Kaulia."

When Lonopele knew that Paao had sailed, he sent against him tempestuous winds and storms, the roaring Kona, with gust following gust, and rain squalls, and the typhoon that tears down villages. And they lost the land, and were driven about without being able to steer, and they drifted into the clouds of imaged shapes and forms. And when the storm was the worst, the fish Aku appeared and assisted them in propelling the canoes; and the fish Opelu, by swimming around the canoes broke the force of the waves and calmed the sea. At length the storm ceased. Then Lonopele looked, and they were not destroyed. So he sent howling winds from the north with driving rain, and they were tossed almost to the stars, and thrown down almost to the bottom of the sea. And when Lonopele saw that they still floated, he sent the Kikahakaiwainapali, a huge bird, to vomit over the canoes, and thus sink them. But Paao had prepared for all of these things when he was making ready for the voyage, and had covered the canoes with matting; so they escaped this danger also.

And Lonopele persevered in his efforts, but Paao escaped every danger. And thenceforth the Aku and the Opelu were sacred in

---

[1] Pola, the raised platform between the two canoes, in double canoes.

the family of Paao, and in the line of his descendants to the time of Hewahewa, the priest of Kamehameha.

After a long and dangerous voyage, he first saw land at Puna, on the island of Hawaii, and there he landed and built a dwelling-place for his God; and he called it the temple of Ahaula. From Puna they coasted along the shore and landed at Puuepa in Kohala. There they built the heiau of Molokini, which is called the temple of Paao.

At that time Hawaii was without chiefs, which thing had lasted for seventeen generations, or I should think for about eight hundred years. There were, indeed, some chiefs, but they did not belong to the line of the royal blood, and this is the reason why the men of Hawaii sought for chiefs in Tahiti, and in other places. During this long period, sometimes men of the people were the rulers, and sometimes there were no rulers, and part of the time they had chiefs from Maui, and from Molokai, and from Oahu, and from Kauai, to govern them. And thus it happened that Pili, who came with Paao from Upolu, became the king of Hawaii, and the progenitor of the Hawaiian line of kings.

And Paao increased in influence and power, and made changes in the religion of the people; he also added two idols, which he brought with him from Upolu, to the number of those worshipped by the Hawaiians.

Paao's descendants held the office of high priest to the time of Kamehameha.

PRODUCTION AND CONSUMPTION OF SUGAR.

SENOR RAMON DE LA SAGRA, the well-known correspondent of the *Diario de la Marina*, furnishes some interesting statistics relative to sugar. The estimates, given in kilogrammes, were carefully made up by M. Dureau from data obtained during the late Exposition in Paris. In 1866, the total product of sugar from cane was 3,159,424,840 lbs., of which Cuba produced for export 1,205,855,560 lbs., and the Hawaiian Islands 17,729,161 lbs. Europe produced 1,490,313,500 lbs. of beet sugar. In 1867, the production was 5,151,289,500 lbs., of which Cuba produced nearly one-third, and the Hawaiian Islands 17,127,187 lbs., or 601,974 lbs. less than the year before.

During 1866, the world consumed 4,305,809,963 lbs. of both beet and cane sugar, of which Great Britain and her colonies used 1,328,020,382 lbs., and the United States 884,000,000 lbs. In 1867, the consumption was 4,497,350,000 lbs., and one-half of this was by the United States and Great Britain and her colonies.

HAWAII AT THE "EXPOSITION UNIVERSELLE," PARIS, 1867.

THE exhibition of Hawaiian products, made at Paris in 1867, being probably the largest ever made outside the Islands, and the most important general evidence in regard to them ever presented to the world, it seems well to arrange some account of the various material forming that evidence.

In the Palace of the Exhibition, Hawaii occupied two square apartments, each measuring fifteen to twenty feet in length and width. These apartments were lined by cases having glazed fronts, and wood-work painted cane-color, and were shaded by cloth canopies suspended above them. In the Park, forming portion of the collective exhibition by the Protestant Missionary Societies, was, also, a valuable display of books relating to Hawaii —mostly published at the Islands, and in the native language. Besides these were many articles of early native manufacture.

Visitors to the Palace were freely offered a printed sheet of four pages, giving in French an account of Hawaii, intended for their information. A translation of this account is here given to show the nature of that information, containing, as it does, some statements that may have novelty to more than one class of readers.

Another, and the chief aid to opinion of this exhibition of Hawaii, is given in a list of persons and articles represented in it. The writer is not aware that such a list has been connectedly published. That following is compiled from the " Catalogue Général," a work of nearly sixteen hundred pages, and the "Authorized English Version," a work of about one thousand pages, professing completeness, but differing much from the former. Through these twenty-six hundred pages is scattered, in sections, the account numbered II., following the description of the Islands translated upon the next four pages, and numbered I.

I.

THE HAWAIIAN ISLANDS.

(Sandwich Islands.)

THE Hawaiian Archipelago is composed of twelve islands situated in the Pacific Ocean, between North America and China, in longitude 157° to 164° west, and latitude 19° to 22° north. These islands are, in going from S.E. to N.W.: Hawaii, capital Hilo, superficies 187 geographical square miles; Maui, cap. Lahaina, sup. 28.49; Molokini, an islet; Kahoolawe, sup. 2.82; Lanai, sup. 4.71; Molokai, sup. 8; Oahu, cap. Honolulu (cap. of the kingdom, about 13,000 inhabitants), sup. 24.69; Kauai, cap. Hanalei, sup. 24.89; Lehua, an islet; Niihau, sup. 3.29; Kaula, an islet. Total superficies, about 285 geographical square miles.

The Soil is in a high degree volcanic, but very fertile. The island of Hawaii has two enormous active volcanoes; Mauna Loa (height = 4,195 mètres [13.763 feet, English], circumference of the crater = 30 kilomètres [about 18⅜ miles, English], depth = 238 mètres [781 feet, English), and Kilauea (circumference of crater = 24 kilomètres, [about 14¼⅜ miles, English], depth, = 330 mètres [1,083 feet, English].

The principal **Mountains** are: Mauna Kea (the White mountain, on account of its cap of perpetual snow), height, 4,250 mètres [13,944 feet, English], Mauna Loa, 4,195 mètres, Hualalai, 3,050 mètres [10,007 feet, English], all the three on the island of Hawaii; and Haleakala, 3,070 mètres [10,072 feet, English], on the island of Maui, presenting a crater, at this time extinct, 50 kilomètres [31.05 miles] in circumference, and more than 600 mètres [1,968 feet, English] in depth. The archipelago possesses numerous streams of water, of which some are navigable by small vessels, and magnificent cascades and hot springs.

The Climate is remarkably healthy and mild. At Honolulu, the temperature, in the shade, varies between $+12°$ and $+32°$ centigrade; the mean is $+21°$. The prevailing wind is the northeast Trade-wind; that blows three out of four days. In winter the southwest wind replaces that of the northeast, and brings great rains. Swamps do not exist.

The Native **Population,** of the same race and of the same language as that peopling all Polynesia, is tall, stout and well made. It has a slightly tawny skin, large eyes, fine forehead, nose a little large at the base, thick lips, glossy hair, commonly black, but sometimes sandy or even brown. It is cheerful, brave and intelligent, and shows a remarkable aptness for the exact sciences.

Constitution. A constitutional hereditary monarchy. Executive power: the king, a privy council, four responsible ministers. Legislative power: the king and the legislative assembly, composed of nobles appointed by the king and representatives elected by all the citizens aged over twenty years knowing how to read and write and possessing a property of one hundred and fifty dollars, or an annual income of seventy-five dollars. The budget is voted for two years. Judiciary power: a supreme court, composed of a supreme judge, chancellor of the kingdom, and of at least two judges; four district courts; police and other tribunals. The constitution guarantees liberty of worship, of the press and of instruction, the right of assembly and of petition, trial by jury and setting at liberty under bail.

Royal Family. The King Kamehameha V., born Dec. 11, 1830, succeeded his brother Kamehameha IV. Nov. 30, 1863. Father of the king, H. H. Kekuanaoa, commander-in-chief. Dowager queens: Kalama, widow of Kamehameha III; Emma, born Jan. 2, 1836, widow of Kamehameha IV.

Cabinet. Minister of Foreign Affairs, M. Crosnier de Varigny, born in France; Interior, Mr. Fred. W. Hutchison, born in Scotland; Finance, Mr. C. C. Harris, born in the United States; Justice, Mr. E. H. Allen, born in the United States.

Religious Worship. Apostolic Vicar, Monseigneur Maigret, Bishop of Arathea, *in partibus;* Anglican Bishop, Staley; President of the American Protestant Mission, the Rev. Titus Coan. (About a quarter of the population belong to the Catholic religion, the remainder is Protestant.)

Diplomatic and Consular Body. The United States maintain at the Hawaiian Islands a resident minister and two consuls; France and Great Britain, each a consul and a commissioner; Belgium, Bremen, Chili, Denmark, Spain, Hamburg, Italy, Lubeck, Oldenburg, the Low Countries, Peru, Prussia, Sweden and Russia, Consuls or Vice-Consuls.

Diplomatic and Consular Agents abroad. The Hawaiian Government has chargés d'affaires in England, the United States, France and Prussia, and consuls at Boston, Oregon City and San Francisco (United States); Falmouth, Liverpool, Ramsgate (England); Australia, Van Diemen's Land, New Zealand, Vancouver's Island (British Colonies); Carlsruhe (Baden); Bremen; Antwerp (Belgium); Valparaiso (Chili); Hongkong (China); Copenhagen (Denmark); Hamburg; Genoa (Italy); Bordeaux, Havre and Marseilles (France); Japan and Peru.

Finances. Public debt, March 31, 1866, $182,974. Budget of expenses for the service of 1866-7: Civil List, $40,000; Endowments, $20,000; Interior (comprising public works), $398,223; Foreign Affairs, $22,600; Finances, $143,995; War, $66,026; Justice, $83,800; Public Instruction, $41,924; Miscellaneous, $42,329; total, $858,897.

Instruction. Teaching is free, and numerous establishments largely diffuse instruction. They all receive subsidies of the State, under the superintendence, and through the care of the Bureau of Education and the Inspector General of Schools. The two chief establishments are the Catholic College of Ahuimanu and that of the American Protestant Mission at Lahainaluna (island of Maui).

The Royal Society of Agriculture publishes from time to time reports of its works.

Institutions for Relief. H. M. Queen Emma has founded near Honolulu, a hospital that bears her name. There exists also an Asylum for the Insane, a Hospital for American seamen, a Lazaretto, a large number of charitable societies, and a Board of Health, presided over by the Minister of the Interior.

Productions, Industry and Commerce. The soil yields all the products of tropical and temperate countries, of which very many are of recent importation. The chief article of food of the natives is the root of the kalo (arum esculentum). Almost all the useful animals have been introduced by Europeans. Sheep, goats, cattle and horses multiply rapidly, and are now very numerous. The pasturage is excellent.

Honolulu has a large sugar refinery, a foundery, with means for making machinery, gas works, mills, etc., and sugar mills are in operation on most of the islands.

The products on which exporting especially relies are: Sugar (export in 1866 for the single port of Honolulu, 17,729,161 pounds, molasses 851,795 gallons), flour, rice (438,367 pounds), coffee (93,682 pounds against 263,705 pounds in 1865), salt (738 tons), cotton (22,289 pounds), goat skins (76,115 bales), hides (282,305 pounds), tallow (159,731 pounds against 179,545 in 1865), pulu, a vegetable down, the product of a fern (212,026 pounds), wool (73,131 pounds against 144,085 in 1865), whale oil (91,182 gallons), whalebone (56,840 pounds), etc. Of other products, silk, tobacco, mats, and woods for cabinet work, serve also to furnish articles of export.

In 1865 the importations were in amount $1,944,265, and the exports $1,808,257, in which the native products came to $1,430,211. Since 1861 especially, Hawaiian commerce has taken a rapid and continuous rise, and the resources of the Islands have developed themselves in very great proportion.

The principal articles of import are: cotton and woolen goods, articles of clothing, coal, castings and iron, tools and machinery, naval outfits, the alimentary conserves of Europe and the spirits of the United States.

Navigation. The Islands possess excellent roadsteads and ports, of which the principal is Honolulu, that are important resorts, especially for whalers. In 1865 one hundred and eighty of these vessels arrived at the various ports, and the export and import commerce was carried on by one hundred and fifty-one merchant vessels, measuring altogether 67,068 tons. There is also a very active coasting trade between the different islands. Finally, the regular line of steamers from San Francisco to China is bound to touch at Honolulu.

About half of the entire commerce is with the United States, and a sixth with Bremen. There exists between that port and Honolulu, a regular line served by Hawaiian vessels.

Weights and Measures. The weights and measures are the same as those of the United States and England, but preparation is being made to adopt the French metrical system. The coins are those of the United States.

Flag. The flag is composed of eight horizontal bands disposed in the following order, from top to bottom: white, red, blue, white, red, blue, white, red, with a blue square at the upper angle towards the staff, traversed by a double red cross bordered with white.

II.

HAWAII.

Exhibitors at the Universal Exhibition at Paris, 1867, according to the corrected Official Catalogues (September Editions), published by authority of the Imperial Commission, and arranged according to the system adopted by that Commission, thus showing the representation of Hawaii in the various departments of production.

Group I. Works of Art.

Class 1. Paintings in Oil. 2. Other Paintings and Drawings. 3

Sculpture, Die-Sinking, Stone and Cameo Engraving. 4. Architectural Designs and Models. 5. Engraving and Lithography.
Represented in
CLASS 3 by
CHASE, H., *Honolulu*. — Photographs of various Landscapes in the Hawaiian Islands; Portrait of H. M. King Kamehameha.

Group II. Apparatus and Application of the Liberal Arts.

Class 6. Printing and Books. 7. Paper Stationery, Binding, Painting and Drawing Materials. 8. Application of Drawing and Modeling to the Common Arts. 9. Photographic Proofs and Apparatus. 10. Musical Instruments. 11. Medical and Surgical Instruments and Apparatus. 12. Mathematical Instruments and Apparatus for Teaching Science. 13. Maps and Geographical and Cosmographical Apparatus.
Represented in
CLASS 6 by
1. EVANGELICAL ASSOCIATION OF HAWAII, *Honolulu*.—Primer; *Huinahelu* (Arithmetic); Hawaiian Bible; Hymn Book; Catechisms; *Hoikehonua* (Geography); *Mooolelo o ka Ekalesia* (History of the Church); New Testament; *Hele Malihini* (Pilgrim's Progress); Sunday School Books; Transactions of the Royal Hawaiian Agricultural Society.
2. DAMON, S. C., *Honolulu*.—The Friend, Bi-monthly Journal.
3. FRANKLIN, Lady, *London*.—"*Ka Buke o ka Pule*" (English Prayer Book), translated by the late King Kamehameha IV.
4. HAWAIIAN GOVERNMENT.—Various Pamphlets; Civil Code and Penal Code; Constitutions of 1841 and 1852; *Ka Hae Hawaii* (The Hawaiian Flag), journal; The Hawaiian Gazette; Collection of laws passed at different periods from 1845 to 1865; *Mooolelo Hawaii* (Hawaiian History); The Polynesian, journal; Hawaiian Reports; The Hawaiian Spectator, journal.
5. GULICK, L. H., *Honolulu*.—*Ka Nupepa Kuokoa* (The Independent Press), illustrated journal.
6. WHITNEY, H. M, *Honolulu*. — *Himeni* (Hymns); Hawaiian-English Dictionary; *Ke Kaao o Laieikawai* (Legend); *Na Huaolelo* (English-Hawaiian Vocabulary); Hawaiian Dictionary.

CLASS 9, see Group I., CHASE, H.
CLASS 12 by
1. CROSNIER DE VARIGNY, *Honolulu*.—Collection of Postage stamps of the country.
CLASS 13 by
1. CROSNIER DE VARIGNY and EM. FÉNARD, *Honolulu*.—Map of the Hawaiian Archipelago, with statistical tables.

2. COLLEGE OF LAHAINALUNA *(island of Maui).*—Map of the Archipelago.

Group III. Furniture and Other Objects for the use of Dwellings.

Class 14. Furniture. 15. Upholstery and Decorative Work. 16. Flint and other Glass; Stained Glass. 17. Porcelain, Earthern ware, and other fancy pottery. 18. Carpets, Tapestry and Furniture Stuffs. 19. Paper Hangings. 20. Cutlery. 21. Gold and Silver Plate. 22. Bronzes and other Artistic Castings and Rapousse Works. 23. Clock and Watchwork. 24. Apparatus and Processes for Heating and Lighting. 25. Perfumery. 26. Leather Work, Fancy Articles and Basket Work.

Represented in
CLASS 14 by
1. HOLDSWORTH, H., *London.*—Table made at Honolulu with the wood of the country.

CLASS 15 by
1. MALUAIKOO, J., *Honolulu.*—Frame decorated with shells.
2. FÉNARD (Emile), *Honolulu.*—Frames of various woods of the country, filled with photographs.

CLASS 18 by
1. H. M. QUEEN EMMA.—Mat twenty-four feet long.
2. FRANKLIN, Lady, *London.*—Mat from the island of Niihau.
3. HAWAIIAN GOVERNMENT.—Mat from Niihau; mat cushions.
4. CROSNIER DE VARIGNY, *Honolulu.*—Mat twenty-one feet by fourteen.
5. HOFFSCHLÆGER & Co., *Honolulu.*—Door mats of cocoa-nut fibre.

CLASS 26 by
1. DOYEN, Mrs.., *Honolulu.*—Basket in shells of the country.

Group IV. Clothing—Including Fabrics—and other Objects worn on the Person.

Class 27. Cotton Yarns, Threads and Tissues. 28. Flaxen and Hempen Yarns, Threads and Tissues. 29. Combed Wool and Worsted Yarns and Fabrics. 30. Carded Wool and Woolen Yarns and Fabrics. 31. Silk and Silk Manufactures. 32. Shawls. 33. Lace, Net, Embroidery and Trimmings. 34. Hosiery, Under-Clothing and Minor Articles. 35. Clothing for both Sexes. 36. Jewelry and Ornaments. 37. Portable Arms. 38. Travelling and Camp Equipage. 39. Toys.

Represented in
CLASS 28 by
1. FRANKLIN, Lady, *London.*—Piece of kapa or tapa, stuff made of beaten bark.

2. HAWAIIAN GOVERNMENT.—Piece of very fine kapa, and mallets with graduated channels used to beat this stuff; pieces of kapa, printed and plain, with bark ready for weaving; beating mallet.

3. H. M. QUEEN EMMA.—Pieces of kapa of different colors; piece of black kapa; mallets for beating this cloth.

CLASS 34 by
1. CROSNIER DE VARIGNY, *Honolulu.*—Canes of cocoa-nut wood and sandal-wood cutters.
2. JUDD, A. F., *Honolulu.*—Canes of cocoa-nut wood.

CLASS 35 by
1. H. M. QUEEN EMMA.—Straw hats; sugar-cane leaf hats; hat straw.
2. FRANKLIN, Lady, *London.*—Two necklaces in red and green feathers of the Oo; Kahili, insignia in feathers, formerly carried before persons of quality in ceremonies; pelerine of Oo feathers (Drepanis pacifica), formerly insignia of very high rank.
3. HERVEY, Lord C., *London.*—Grand royal mantle of Oo feathers.
4. HAWAIIAN GOVERNMENT. — Hair necklace, worn formerly by chiefs; sacred vase, about one hundred years old, carried formerly by chiefs as a talisman; Oo feather necklace; model of native hut, made of leaves of the pandanus, with mat covering the ground.
5. HOLDSWORTH, H., *London.*—Necklace.

CLASS 37 by
1. HAWAIIAN GOVERNMENT.—Javelin wood of Kauwila (*alphitonia excelsa*).

Group V. Products, Raw and Manufactured, of Mining, Industry, Forestry, etc.

Class 40. Mining and Metallurgy. 41. Forest Products and Industries. 42. Products of the Chase and Fisheries; Uncultivated Products. 43. Agricultural Products (not used as food) easily preserved. 44. Chemical and Pharmaceutical Products. 45. Specimens of the Chemical Processes used in Bleaching, Dyeing, Printing and Dressing. 46. Leather and Skins.

Represented in

CLASS 40 by
1. CROSNIER DE VARIGNY, Minister of Foreign Affairs, *Honolulu.*—Collection of volcanic products; sulphur, lava, pumice-stone, stalagmites and silky fibres from the volcanoes of Mauna Loa and Kilauea.
2. H. M. QUEEN EMMA.—Common gourds and calabashes, gourds and calabashes with designs.

CLASS 41 by
1. FISCHER, W., *Honolulu.*—Specimens of various woods suitable for cabinet work.

2. HASSLOCHER, E. (Hawaiian Consul), *Carlsruhe.*—Specimens of wood for cabinet making.
3. HAWAIIAN GOVERNMENT.—Large gourd, with its cover; bottle gourd; calabashes for domestic use; vessels in hard wood; fan made of plaited leaf and sandals of bark fibre.

CLASS 42 by
1. HAWAIIAN GOVERNMENT.—Fibres and fabric of native barks; *pulu*, vegetable down obtained from a fern.
2. PEASE (W. HARPER) *Honolulu.*—Collection of Hawaiian shells.

CLASS 43 by
1. ELBING, *Honolulu.*—Tobacco and cigars.
2. FORD, S. P., *Honolulu.*—Sea Island Cotton.
3. JANION, R. C., Hawaiian Consul at Liverpool.—Specimens of Hawaiian wool.
4. JANION, GREEN & Co., *Waimea.*—Washed wool.

Group VI. Apparatus and Processes used in the Common Arts.

CLASSES 47 to 66 inclusive. Represented in
CLASS 49 [Implements used in the Chase, Fisheries, and Gathering Wild Products] by
1. HAWAIIAN GOVERNMENT.—Bark fibre net; netting shuttle; line and hook in mother of pearl and bone; small harpoon in iron-wood.

CLASS 56 [Apparatus and Processes used in Weaving] by
1. H. M. QUEEN EMMA.—Blocks used for printing kapa.
2. HARTBOSTEE, ISAAC, *Island of Maui.*—Blocks used for printing kapa.

CLASS 65 by
1. HAWAIIAN GOVERNMENT. — Wooden adze with stone cutting edge.

CLASS 66 [Navigation and Life Boats; Yachts and Pleasure Boats] by
1. H. M. QUEEN EMMA.—Model of double canoe.
2. HAWAIIAN GOVERNMENT.—Model of double canoe, with deck made of network, with its paddles.
3. HOLDSWORTH, H., *London.*—Two models of canoes.

Group VII. Food, Fresh or Preserved, in Various States of Preservation.

Class 67. Cereals and other Farinaceous Products, with their Derivatives. 68. Bread and Pastry. 69. Fatty Substances used as Food, Milk and Eggs. 70. Meat and Fish. 71. Vegetables and Fruit. 72. Condiments and Stimulants; Sugar and Confectionery. 73. Fermented Drinks.

Represented in
CLASS 67 by
1. HONOLULU RICE MILL.—Rice grown from South Carolina seed, gathered in the island of Hawaii and prepared at the factory of Honolulu, 25th March, 1866; Arrowroot, Tapioca.
2. SAVIDGE, S., *Honolulu.*—Arrowroot, tapioca.
3. JANION, GREEN & CO., *Honolulu.*—Arrowroot of Waiaha, island of Hawaii.

CLASS 72 by
1. BALL & ADAM, *Wailuku, Island of Maui.*—Sugar.
2. HAWAIIAN GOVERNMENT.—Roots of the *awa (Macropiper methysticum)*.
3. HOFFSCHLŒGER & Co., *Honolulu.*—Kona coffee in shell.
4. JANION, GREEN & CO., *Honolulu.*—Sugars.
5. SAVIDGE, S., *Honolulu.*— Coffee of Kona, island of Hawaii; sugars.

Group VIII. Live Stock, and Specimens of Agricultural Buildings.

Not represented.

Group IX. Live Produce, and Specimens of Horticultural Works.

Not represented.

Group X. Articles exhibited with the special object of improving the physical and moral condition of the people.

Classes 89 to 95, inclusive and concluding.
Represented in
CLASS 89 [Apparatus and methods used in the Instruction of Children] by

HAWAIIAN GOVERNMENT.—Books for Education: *Kumumua* (Primer); *Hoailonahelu* (Algebra); *Huinahelu* (Arithmetic); *Helunaau, Helukamalii* (Mental Arithmetic); *Lira Hawaii, Lira kamalii* (Hymns); *Alakaimua* (Primer); *Ui no ke Akua* (Catechism); *Hoikehonua* (Geography); *Palapalaaina* (Atlas); *Olelo Hoakaka no ka Honua* (Questions in Geography); *Anahonua* (Geometry); Hawaiian Grammar, by Andrews; Dictionary, Hawaiian and English; Vocabulary, English and Hawaiian; *Mooolelo Hawaii* (Hawaiian History); New Testament; *Ao kiko* (Punctuation).

[Many samples of sugars, from different plantations, were exhibited, that do not appear upon this catalogue. Missionary Societies also exhibited in the Park, as described hereafter.]

In the Park, situated in its universal confusion, or perhaps cosmopolitan assemblage of the works of almost every variety of humanity for almost every variety of purpose, all in strange proximity, was the building forming the Exhibition Hall of the Evangelical Missionary Societies of the World,—a building having for neighbors on its four sides a club house, a large collection of the latest weapons of war, a Mexican idol-temple, and "Allée de Washington,"—a compliment to America,—and also a tramway. In this building the London Missionary Society showed the principal war-god of Kamehameha I., a red-feathered head with very long, slant, pearl-shell eyes and unaimiable aspect. Near it the "American Board" showed two cases. One presented many idols and other heathenish productions, and was labelled "Hawaii, 1816." The other presented many books and sheets, printed mostly, if not entirely, in native language, and was marked "Hawaii, 1866." The "Board" had there, for distribution, an octavo tract of eight pages, containing a sketch of its operations, and the following allusions:—

"As the people of the Hawaiian Islands, through the efforts of the American Board, were brought up from the condition of savage barbarism to a place among Christian nations, a few specimens are exhibited of the idols formerly worshipped, and of the various implements once in use, now happily matters of history." The Board exhibited about eight hundred different publications in nearly forty languages (out of two thousand works issued by its presses), and of these this Hawaiian collection was a conspicuous portion. The Religious Tract Society of London published an account of the Mission Exhibitors, with a reference to Hawaii similar to that just given.

For description of awards see Hawaiian Gazette.

[1] The first edition of the official Catalogue of Exhibitors awarded prizes by the International Jury, reports the two following:—

Class 6. Bronze medal, to Printing Establishment of the Hawaiian Government at Honolulu, for official documents and journals.

Classes 89, 90. Silver Medal to Hawaiian Kingdom for reports and documents.

[1] A Gold Medal was awarded to the Hawaiian Government.

ISLANDS OF THE NORTH PACIFIC.

From the Report of the Honolulu Harbor Master, Capt. Daniel Smith, the following corrected positions have been extracted. Capt. Smith has compiled the list from various sources, principally from Lieut. Brooke of the U. S. Schooner *Fennimore Cooper*, Capt. Brookes of the *Gambia*, Capts. Paty, Long, Stone and Tengström, and also from many whalers' log books. The list of the Gilbert, Marshall, and Caroline Islands was arranged by Dr. L. H. Gulick, who resided at Ebon for ten years. In all cases where the islands are inhabited, the native names have been adopted where known, for otherwise it would be a most difficult task to arrange the synonyms, as each Reef, Atoll or Island, has been renamed many times.

ISLANDS NORTHWEST OF THE HAWAIIAN GROUP.

Bird Island (534 ft. high), 23° 06′ N. lat., 161° 57′ W. long. West of Greenwich. Lieut. Brooke, U. S. N.

Neckar Island (280 ft. high), 23° 35′ N. lat., 164° 39′ W. long. Lieut. Brooke, U. S. N.

French Frigate Shoal, S. E. extremity, 23° 44′ N. lat., 166° 04′ W. long.; N. W. extremity, 23° 52′ N. lat., 166° 22′ W. long.; S. W. extremity, 23° 42′ N. lat., 166° 20′ W. long.; Islet on Reef, 23° 46′ N. lat., 166° 17′ W. long. Capt. Brooks, bark *Gambia*. Lieut. Brooke, U. S. N.

Gardner's Island and Rocks (170 ft. high), 25° 01′ N. lat., 167° 59′ W. long. Lieut. Brooke.

Maro Reef (breakers), extending six miles N. N. W. and S. S. E., 25° 31′ N. lat., 170° 37½′ W. long. Lieut. Brooke.

Laysan Island (centre), 25° 48′ N. lat., 171° 42′ W. long. Lieut. Brooke.

Bank (soundings 15, 17, 20 and 40 fathoms), 25° 36′ N. lat., 173° 20′ W. long. Lieut. Brooke.

Lisiansky, 26° 03′ N. lat., 173° 42′ W. long. Capt. Paty and others.

Brooks', Middleton or Massachusetts Island, 28° 13′ N. lat., 177° 23′ W. long. Capt. Brooks. A depot placed here by the Pacific Mail Co., 1867. H. M. Whitney.

Pearl and Hermes Reef (circumference of the shoals 42 miles), N. E. point 27° 56′ N. lat., 175° 45′ W. long. Various authorities (mean).

Bunker's or Philadelphia Island, 28° 00′ N. lat., 173° 30′ W. long. Not yet certain.

Ocean, Cure, Staver's Island, 28° 25′ N. lat., 178° 30′ W. long. Various authorities (mean).

Krusenstern Rock, 22° 15′ N. lat., 175° 37′ W. long. Admiral Krusenstern.

Delaware Reef or Shoal, 27° 30′ N. lat., 174° 30′ W. long. Very doubtful.

Two Brothers. Very doubtful. Lieut. Brooke, U. S. N., Captain Brooks, and Captain Paty.

GUANO ISLANDS.

Johnson, Smith or Cornwallis Island, 16° 45′ N. lat., 169° 30′ W. long. Lieut. Brooke. 16° 45′ N. lat., 169° 46′ W. long. By various others (mean).

Howland's Island, 00° 48′ N. lat., 176° 83′ W. long. By Capt. Chisholm, well ascertained.

Baker's Island, 00° 13′ N. lat., 176° 22′ W. long. Mr. C. A. Williams, well ascertained.

MICRONESIAN ISLANDS.

Arorai, Hope or Hurd's Island, S. point, 2° 41′ S. lat., 177° 01′ E. long.; N. point, 2° 37′ S. lat., 176° 57′ E. long. M. Dutaillis in Findlay's Directory.

Tamana, Chase or Phebe Island, centre, 2° 35′ S. lat., 176° 15′ E. long. Capt. Veranus Smith. S. point, 2° 28′ S. lat., 176° 00′ E. long. Capt. Handy.

Oneke, Clerk, Rotch or Eliza's Island, centre, 1° 50′ S. lat., 175° 30′ E. long. Capt. V. Smith. Centre, 1° 55′ S. lat., 175° 49′ E. long. Capt. Handy.

Nukunau, or Byron's Island, centre, 1° 25′ S. lat., 176° 45′ E. long. Capt. V. Smith. Centre, 1° 25′ S. lat., 176° 35′ E. long. Capt. Handy.

Peru, Francis or Maria Island, centre, 1° 25′ S. lat., 176° 15′ E. long. Capt. V. Smith. Centre, 1° 15′ S. lat., 176° 00′ E. long. Capt. Handy.

Tapitouwea, Drummond or Bishop Island, S. E. point, 1° 28′ S. lat., 175° 13′ E. long.; N. W. point, 1° 08′ S. lat., 174° 50′ E. long. Wilkes' chart.

Nonouti, Sydenham's or Blaney's Island, S. E. point, 0° 45′ S. lat., 174° 30′ E. long.; S. W. point, 0° 45′ S. lat., 174° 23′ E. long.; N. point, 0° 30′ S. lat., 174° 20′ E. long.; W. point, 0° 35′ S. lat., 174° 15′ E. long. Wilkes' chart.

Aranuka, or Henderville's Island, S. point, 0° 10′ N. lat., 173° 40½′ E. long.; N. E. point, 0° 13½′ N. lat., 173° 41½′ E. long.; W. point, 0° 11½′ N. lat., 173° 35½′ E. long. Wilkes' chart.

Kuria, or Woodle's Island, S. point, 0° 12′ N. lat., 173° 27½′ E. long.; N. point, 0° 17′ N. lat., 173° 26½′ E. long. Wilkes' chart. Centre, 0° 14′ N. lat., 173° 27′ E. long. Capt. Handy.

Apamama, or Hopper's Island, S. W. point, 0° 26′ N. lat., 173° 51′ E. long.; S. E. point, 0° 21′ N. lat., 174° 01′ E. long.; N. W. point, 0° 30½′ N. lat., 173° 54′ E. long. Wilkes' chart.

Maiana, Gilbert's or Hall's Island, N. point, 1° 02′ N. lat., 173° 04′ E. long.; S. point, 0° 51′ N. lat., 173° 03½′ E. long.; E. point, 0° 58′ N. lat., 173° 08′ E. long.; W. point, 0° 55′ N. lat., 172° 59′ E. long. Wilkes' chart. Centre, 0° 58′ N. lat., 173° 06′ E. long. Capt. Handy.

Apaiang, or Charlotte's Island, S. point, 1° 44′ N. lat., 173° 07′ E. long.; N. point, 1° 58′ N. lat., 172° 59′ E. long.; N. W. point, 1° 54′ N. lat., 172° 55′ E. long. Wilkes' chart. Centre, 1° 50′ F. lat., 173° 04′ E. long. Capt. Handy.

Tarawa, or Knoy's Island, S. E. point, 1° 22′ N. lat., 173° 12′ E. long.; S. W. point, 1° 22′ N. lat., 173° 00′ E. long.; N. point, 1° 29′ N. lat., 173° 03′ E. long. Wilkes' chart. Centre, 1° 30′ N. lat., 173° 06′ E. long. Capt. Handy.

Marakei, or Matthew's Island, middle S. point, 1° 58′ N. lat., 173° 25½′ E. long.; N. point, 2° 03′ M. lat., 173° 34′ E. long.; centre, 2° 00′ N. lat., 173° 25′ E. long. Capt. Handy.

Butaritari, or Touching Island, S. point, 3° 01′ N. lat., 172° 45′ E. long.; N. E. point, 3° 10′ N. lat., 172° 56′ E. long.; N. W. point, 3° 13′ N. lat., 172° 40′ E. long. Wilkes' chart. Centre, 3° 08′ N. lat., 172° 50′ E. long. Capt. Handy.

— 31 —

Makin, or Pitt's Island, N. W. point, 3° 20′ N. lat., 172° 57′ E. long. Wilkes' chart. Centre, 3° 20′ N. lat., 172° 50′ E. long. Capt. Handy.
Banabe, or Ocean Island, centre, 0° 52′ S. lat., 169° 50′ E. long. Capt. Handy. Centre, 0° 52′ S. lat., 168° 24½′ E. long. M. Dutaillis. Centre, 0° 48′ S. lat., 169° 49′ E. long. Capt. Cheyne. Centre, 0° 50′ S. lat., 169° 45′ E. long. Capt. V. Smith.
Nawodo, or Pleasant Island, centre, 0° 25′ S. lat., 167° 05′ E. long. Capt. Handy. Centre, 0° 25′ S. lat., 167° 05′ E. long. Capt. Cheyne. Centre, 0° 25′ S. lat., 167° 20′ E. long. Capt. V. Smith.

RATACK ISLANDS.

Milli, or Mulgrave Island, S. W. point, 6° 09′ N. lat., 171° 30′ E. long.; N. W. point, 6° 20′ N. lat., 171° 28′ E. long. Duperry. Tokowa Islet, 6° 15′ N. lat., 171° 56′ E. long. Dutaillis. Jabunwuni, 6° 20′ N. lat., 171° 52′ E. long.; S. E. point, 5° 58′ N. lat., 172° 02½′ E. long. Capt. Brown. S. E. point, 5° 59′ N. lat., 172° 02′ E. long. U. S. Ex. Ex.
Majuro, or Arrowsmith's Island, S. E. point, 7° 05′ N. lat., 171° 23′ E. long. U. S. Ex. Ex. W. point, 7° 15′ N. lat., 171° 00′ E. long. Capt. Brown.
Arhno, Daniel or Peddlar's Island, N. E. point, 7° 30′ N. lat., 171° 55′ E. long.; S. W. point, 7° 11′ N. lat., 171° 40′ E. long. U. S. Ex. Ex.
Aurh, or Ibbetson's Island, N. E. point, 8° 18′ N. lat., 171° 12′ E. long. Kotzebue.
Maloelab, or Calvert Island, S. E. point, 8° 29′ N. lat., 171° 11′ E. long.; N. W. Islet, 8° 54′ N. lat., 170° 49′ E. long. Kotzebue.
Erikub, or Bishop Junction Island, S. E. point, 9° 06′ N. lat., 170° 04′ E. long. Kotzebue.
Wotje or Otdia, or Romanzoff Island, anchorage within the N. W. point, 9° 33′ N. lat., 170° 10′ E. long.; E. point, 9° 23′ N. lat., 170° 16′ E. long. Kotzebue.
Likieb, or Count Heiden Island, centre of group, 9° 51½′ N. lat., 169° 13½′ E. long.; N. W. point, 10° 63′ N. lat., 169° 01′ E. long. Kotzebue.
Jemo, or Steeple Island, center, 9° 58′ N. lat., 169° 45′ E. long. Kotzebue.
Ailuck, or Tindall or Watt's Island, N. point, 10° 27′ N. lat., 170° 00′ E. long. Kotzebue.
Mejit, Miadi, or New Year's Island, centre, 10° 08′ N. lat., 170° 56′ E. long. Kotzebue.
Utirik, or Button Island, centre, 11° 20′ N. lat., 169° 50′ E. long. Capt. Brown.
Taka, or Souworoff Island, centre, 11° 05′ N. lat., 169° 40′ E. long. Capt. Brown.
Bikar, or Dawson's Island, middle of group, 11° 48′ N. lat., 170° 07′ E. long. Kotzebue.

RALICK ISLANDS.

Ebon, or Boston Island, centre, 4° 39′ N. lat., 168° 50′ E. long. Hazemeister. Centre, 4° 30′ N. lat., 168° 42′ E. long. Capt. Cheyne. Centre, 4° 34′ N. lat., 168° 45′ E. long. Capt. Handy. Anchorage within S. W. point, 4° 39′ N. lat., 168° 49′ E. long. Capt. Brown.
Namorik, or Baring's Island, centre, 5° 35′ N. lat., 168° 18′ E. long. Capt. Handy.
Kili, or Hunter's Island, centre, 5° 46′ N. lat., 169° 00′ E. long. Capt. Dennet. Centre, 5° 40′ N. lat., 169° 15′ E. long. Capt. Handy.
Jaluit, or Bonham's Island, W. point, 6° 00′ N. lat., 169° 30′ E. long.; N. point, 6° 17′ N. lat., 169° 10′ E. long. Duperrey's Chart. N. point, 6° 22′ N. lat., 169° 22′ E. long.; S. pt. 5° 47′ N. lat., 169° 36′ E. long. Capt. Brown.

Ailinglablab or Muskillo Group, S. point, 7° 15ʹ N. lat., 163° 40ʹ E. long.; S. point, middle lobe, 7° 46ʹ N. lat., 168° 23ʹ E. long.; Isthmus containing N. and middle point, 8° 00ʹ N. lat., 168° 13ʹ E. long.; N. point, 8° 10ʹ N. lat., 168° 00ʹ E. long. Capt. Cramchenko in Findlay.

Jabwat or Tebut, centre, 8° 25ʹ N. lat., 168° 17ʹ E. long. Kotzebue.
Lib, or Princessa Island, centre, 8° 20ʹ N. lat., 167° 30ʹ E. long. Capt. Dennet.
[1] Namo, or Margaretta Island, S. extremity, 8° 55ʹ N. lat., 167° 42ʹ E. long.
[1] Kwajalen, or Catherine Island, N. Islet, 9° 14ʹ N. lat., 167° 02ʹ E. long.
Lae, or Brown's Island, centre, 9° 00ʹ N. lat., 166° 20ʹ E. long. Capt. Brown.
[1] Ujae, or Lydia Island, centre, 9° 04ʹ N. lat., 165° 58ʹ E. long. Ship Ocean.
[1] Wotto, or Shanz Island, centre, 10° 05ʹ N. lat., 166° 04ʹ E. long. Capt. Shanz.
Ailinginae, or Remski-Korsakoff Island, S. W. point, 11° 08ʹ N. lat., 166° 20ʹ E. long.; S. W. point, 11° 08ʹ N. lat., 166° 26½ʹ E. long. U. S. Ex. Ex.
Rongerik Island, E. point, 11° 26½ʹ N. lat., 167° 14½ʹ E. long. Kotzebue. Centre, 11° 14ʹ N. lat., 166° 35ʹ E. long. U. S. Ex. Ex.
Rongelab, or Pescadores Islands, centre, 11° 19ʹ N. lat., 167° 35ʹ E. long. Kotzebue. Centre, 11° 20ʹ N. lat., 167° 30ʹ E. long. U. S. Ex. Ex.
[1] Bikeni, or Escachottz Island, W. point, 11° 40ʹ N. lat., 166° 24ʹ E. long. (165° 24ʹ) Kotzebue. Centre of S. point, 11° 33ʹ N. lat., 165° 37ʹ E. long. Capt. Brown. W. part, 11° 59ʹ N. lat., 165° 00ʹ E. long. Duperrey's Chart.
Eniwetok, or Brown's Islands, Parry's Islet, 11° 21ʹ N. lat., 162° 52ʹ E. long. Horsburg. N. point, 11° 40ʹ N. lat., 161° 05ʹ E. long.; centre S. line, 11° 20ʹ N. lat., 161° 05ʹ E. long. Lutke's Chart.
Ujilong, or Morning Star Group, centre, 9° 52ʹ N. lat., 160° 56ʹ E. long. Capt. James.
Ujilong, or Kewley Group, S. end, 9° 47ʹ N. lat., 161° 15ʹ E. long. Capt. Kewley.
Merrel Island or Bank, 29° 57ʹ N. lat., 174° 31ʹ E. long., (doubtful). Lieut. Raper's Epitome.
Byers Island, Patrocinio, 26° 09ʹ N. lat., 175° 48ʹ E. long., (doubtful). Raper.
Rico-de-Oro, 29° 51ʹ N. lat., 157° 04ʹ E. long., (doubtful). Raper.
Broughton Rocks, 345 ft. high, 33° 38ʹ N. lat., 139° 16ʹ E. long. U. S. Exploring Expedition.
Fatsizio Island, middle, 33° 06ʹ N. lat., 140° E. long. Raper.
South Island, 32° 30ʹ N. lat., 140° 03ʹ E. long. Krusenstern and Raper.
Ponafidin Island or Rock, 30° 30ʹ N. lat., 140° 06ʹ E. long. Lieut. Ponafidin.
Bayonaise Island or Rock, 32° 01ʹ N. lat., 140° E. long. French frigate Bayonaise.
Smith Island or Rock, 31° 18ʹ N. lat., 139° 50ʹ E. long. H. M. S. Tribune.
Sail Rock, or Lot's Wife, 29° 47ʹ N. lat., 140° 22ʹ E. long. U. S. S. Macedonia.
Malabriga Islands, 27° 20ʹ N. lat., 145° 25ʹ E. long. Raper, (doubtful position).
Grampus Islands, 25° 10ʹ N. lat., 146° 40ʹ E. long. Raper, (doubtful position).

VOLCANO ISLANDS.

Sulphur Island, volcanic, 24° 48ʹ N. lat., 141° 20ʹ E. long. Raper.
Reef, volcanic, 24° 48ʹ N. lat., 141° 24ʹ E. long. Napoleon 3d, whaler.
San Alesandro Island, volcanic, 25° 14ʹ N. lat., 141° 18ʹ E. long. Raper.
Dionisio Island, volcanic, 24° 22ʹ N. lat., 141° 28ʹ E. long. Raper.

[1] These Islands require further examination.

BONIN ISLANDS, EXTENDING NORTH AND SOUTH FORTY-TWO MILES.

Parry's Group, North Rock, 27° 45ʹ N. lat., 142° 07ʹ E. long. Raper.
Kater Island, North Rock, 27° 31ʹ N. lat., 142° 12ʹ E. long. Raper.
Peel Island, south-west Islet, 27° 02ʹ N. lat., 142° 10ʹ E. long. Raper.
Port Lloyd (Peel Island), 27° 06ʹ N. lat., 142° 11ʹ E. long. Raper.
Bailey Islands, south Islet, 28° 30ʹ N. lat., 142° 13ʹ E. long. Raper. Raper (not well ascertained).
Rosario Island, 27° 16ʹ N. lat., 140° 50ʹ E. long. Raper, (not well ascertained).
Kendrick Island, 24° 35ʹ N. lat., 134° E. long. Raper, (not well ascertained).

Rosa Island, 24° 28ʹ N. lat., 130° 40ʹ E. long. Raper, (not well ascertained).
Borodino Islands, north one, 26° 02ʹ N. lat., 131° 15ʹ E. long. Raper.
Parece Vella, Sail Rock, 20° 30ʹ N. lat., 136° 06ʹ E. long. Capt. Douglass.
Barras Rock, 21° 42ʹ N. lat., 140° 55ʹ E. long. Capt. Barras, Mary Ann.
Lindsay Rock, 19° 20ʹ N. lat., 141° 20ʹ E. long. Capt. Lindsay, Amelia.
Cornwallis, Smyth, Sybilla, Petrel or Gaspar Rico Reef, with Islets S. S. E. and N. N. W., 20 miles; northermost clump of rocks in lat. 14° 41ʹ N., long. 168° 56ʹ E. long. Lieut. Brooke, U. S. N.
Halcyon or Wake's Island, on which the Libelle was wrecked in 1866, entrance to lagoon boat-passage, 19° 19ʹ N. lat., 160° 30ʹ E. long. This Island or reef is placed in 19° 11ʹ N. lat. by the U. S. Exploring Expedition, but by Capt. Wood, Capt. Cargill and Capt. English, who have just visited the wreck, as above, viz.: 19° 19ʹ N. lat., 160° 30ʹ E. long. Low; about seven miles long. W. T. Brigham.
Marcus Island is marked doubtful on most charts, but Capt. Gillett, in the Morning Star, in 1864, passed near an Island in lat. 24° 04ʹ N.; long. 154° 02ʹ E.
Marshall or Jardine Islands, (2 small), 21° 40ʹ N. lat., 151° 35ʹ E. long. Some whalemen affirm that they have landed on these rocks; others assert that they have sailed over this position without seeing anything.
Assumption Island, 2000 ft. high, 19° 41ʹ N. lat., 145° 27ʹ E. long. Raper.
Uraccas Rocks, 20° 10ʹ N. lat., 145° 25ʹ E. long. Raper.
Faralon Island, 20° 30ʹ N. lat., 145° 12ʹ long. Spanish Corvette Narvaez.
Guy Rock, 20° 30ʹ N. lat., 145° 30ʹ E. long. Raper.
Grigan Island, 18° 48ʹ N. lat., 145° 40ʹ E. long. Raper.
Pagan Island, 18° 15ʹ N. lat., 145° 48ʹ E. long. Raper.
The last three positions are not well ascertained.

CAROLINE GROUP.

Ualan, Kusaie or Strong's Island, centre, 5° 19ʹ N. lat., 163° 06ʹ E. long. Lutke's chart. Coquillo harbor, N. E. Islet, 5° 21ʹ N. lat., 163° 01ʹ E. long. Duperrey's chart. Port Lolin, south, N. E. Islet, 5° 15ʹ N. lat., 163° 05ʹ E. long.; weather harbor, 5° 19½ʹ N. lat., 163° 09ʹ E. long. Lutke's chart. Centre, 5° 20ʹ N. lat., 162° 54ʹ E. long. Spanish chart, by D. F. Coello, Mad., 1852.
Pingelap or McAskill Islands, north Islet, 6° 13ʹ N. lat., 160° 47ʹ E. long.; south Islet, 6° 12ʹ N. lat., 160° 47½ʹ E. long. Captain Duperrey. Centre, 6° 13½ʹ N. lat., 160° 48ʹ E. long. Captain Cheyne.
Tugulu or McAskill Islands, centre, 6° 13ʹ N. lat., 160° 50ʹ E. long. Spanish chart.

Mokil or Duperrey's Islands, N. E. point, 6° 42′ N. lat., 159° 50′ E. long. Duperrey's chart. Centre, 6° 40′ N. lat., 159° 49′ E. long. Captain Cheyne.

Aura or Duperrey's Islands, centre, 6° 40′ N. lat., 159° 47′ E. long. Spanish chart.

Ponapi, Quirosa or Ascension isles, Ronkiti harbor, 6° 48′ N. lat., 158° 19′ E. long. Lutke's chart. 6° 48′ N. lat., 158° 14′ E. long. Captain Cheyne. 6° 48′ N. lat., 158° 30′ E. long. Average observations by several whale Captains. Ponatik harbor, 6° 48′ N. lat., 158° 30′ E. long. Lutke's chart. 6° 50′ N. lat., 158° 28′ E. long. Captain Walker. 6° 48′ N. lat., 158° 40′ E. long. Captain Chase.

Bonabe or Ascension isles, Ronkiti harbor, 6° 48′ N. lat., 158° 19′ E. long. Spanish chart.

Andema or Frazer Islands, centre, 6° 42′ N. lat., 158° 05′ E. long. Spanish chart.

Ant, Frazer's or William 4th's Group, N. E. part, 6° 42′ N. lat., 158° 03′ E. long. Captain Cheyne. Extreme south, 6° 43½′ N. lat., 158° 05½′ E. long. Lutke's chart.

Pakin, centre, 7° 10′ N. lat., 157° 43′ E. long. Captain Cheyne. S. E. Islet, 7° 02′ N. lat., 158° 00½′ E. long.; W. point, 7° 05′ N. lat. 157° 56½′ E. long. Captain Lutke.

Pagnema, centre, 7° 02′ N. lat., 157° 49′ E. long. Spanish chart.

Ngatik, Los Valientes or seven Islands, extreme E., 5° 47½′ N. lat., 157° 32′ E. long. Lutke in Findlay. S. E. Islet, 5° 47′ N. lat., 157° 32′ E. long.; N. Islet, 5° 51′ N. lat., 157° 29′ E. long.; W. Islet, 5° 47′ N. lat., 157° 22′ E. long. Lutke's chart. W. Islet, 5° 40′ N. lat., 157° 14′ E. long. Captain Cheyne.

Ngaric Islands, centre, 5° 47′ N. lat., 157° 27′ E. long. Spanish chart.

Oruluk, San Augustino and Baxo Trista, centre of Bordelaise Island, 7° 39′ N. lat., 155° 05′ E. long.; Jane Island, 7° 33′ N. lat., 155° 03′ E. long.; Larkin's Island, N. E. point, 7° 36′ N. lat., 155° 10′ E. long. Findlay. Meaburn's Island, 7° 49′ N. lat., 155° 20′ E. long. Norie's chart. San Agustin reef, S. E. end dangerous, 7° 11′ N. lat., 156° 08′ E. long.; N. W. end dangerous, 7° 26′ N. lat., 155° 57′ E. long.; Bordelaise Island, N. W. end of reef, 7° 26′ N. lat., 155° 58′ E. long. Spanish chart.

Dunkin's shoal, (doubtful) south end, 9° 50′ N. 154° 10′ E. long. Findlay. North end, 9° 17′ N. lat., 154° 29′ E. long. Spanish chart.

Nukuor or Monteverde Islands, centre, 3° 27′ N. lat., 155° 48′ E. long. Findlay.

Dunkin's Island, centre, 3° 57′ N. lat., 154° 34′ E. long. Captain Aikin.

Nuguor, centre, 3° 50′ N. lat., 154° 56′ E. long. Spanish chart.

Sotoane or Mortlock Islands, south point, 5° 17′ N. lat., 153° 46′ E. long.; S. E. point, 5° 19′ N. lat., 153° 51′ E. long.; west point, 5° 27′ N. lat., 153° 36′ E. long. Lutke's chart. N. W. extreme, 5° 27′ N. lat., 153° 24′ E. long.; S. W. extreme, 5° 08′ N. lat., 153° 38′ E. long. Captain Cheyne.

Lugunor or Mortlock Islands, east point, 5° 30′ N. lat., 153° 59′ E. long. Lutke's chart. Centre, 5° 39′ N. lat., 153° 32′ E. long. Captain Cheyne. West point, 5° 30′ N. lat., 153° 52′ E. long. Lutke's chart. Port Chamisso, 5° 29′ N. lat., 153° 38′ E. long. Lutke in Findlay.

Eatal, south point, 5° 33′ N. lat., 153° 43′ E. long.; north point, 5° 37′ N. lat., 153° 43′ E. long. Lutke's chart.

Lugunor, Etal, north end, 5° 35′ N. lat., 153° 41′ E. long.; N. E. end, 5° 28′ E. long.; Ta, S. E. end, 5° 16′ N. lat., 153° 51′ E. long.; N. W. end, 5° 30′ N. lat., 153° 34′ E. long. Spanish chart.

Namoluk or Skiddy's Group, N. W. Islet, 5° 55′ N. lat., 153° 13½′ E. long. Lutke in Findlay. 5° 55′ E. lat., 153° 17′ E. long. Lutke's chart.

Namulùe or Skiddy's Group, centre, 5° 55′ N. lat., 153° 14′ E. long. Spanish chart.

Mokor or Hash Island, centre (?) 5° 42′ N. lat., 152° 43′ E. long. Blunt's chart.
Losap, Lounsappe or D'Urville's island, centre, 7° 3′ N. lat., 152° 42′ E. long. Duperrey in Findlay. 7° 5′ N. lat., 152° 37′ E. long. D'Urville's chart.
Rafael island, centre, 7° 18′ N. lat., 153° 54′ E. long. Raper.
Luasap or D'Urville's Island, centre, 6° 50′ N. lat., 152° 39′ Spanish chart.
Truk or Hogoleu Islands and Reefs, S. point, 6° 58′ N. lat., 151° 56′ E. long. (Or Ruc atoll), E. point, 7° 10′ N. lat., 151° 57′ E. long. W. point, 7° 10′ N. lat., 151° 21′ E. long. D'Urville's chart. N. point, 7° 43 N. lat., 151° 43′ E. long.
Royalist Island, S. extreme, 6° 47′ N. lat., 152° 8′ E. long. Captain Cheyne.
Ruc or Hogoleu or Bergh's Islands or Reefs, S. point, 6° 57′ N. lat., 151° 54′ E. long. N. point, 7° 43′ N. lat., 151° 39′ E. long.; W. point, 7° 20′ N. lat., 151° 19′ E. long. Spanish chart.
Morileu or Hall's Islands, N. E. Islet, 8° 42′ N. lat., 152° 26′ E. long.; S. W. Islet, 8° 36′ N. lat., 152° 07′ E. long. Lutke's chart. N. E. end, 8° 42′ N. lat., 152° 29′ E. long.; S. W. end, 8° 32′ North lat., 152° 03′ E. long. Spanish chart.
Namolipiafane, N. E. Islet, 8° 34′ N. lat., 152° 01′ E. long.; S. Islet, 8° 25′ N. lat., 151° 50′ E. long. Lutke's chart. S. W. Islet, 8° 30′ N. lat., 151° 42½′ E. long. Lutke in Findlay.
Namolipiafan, centre, 8° 32′ N. lat., 151° 54′ E. long. Spanish Chart.
Faiu, East, or Lutke's Island, centre, 8° 33′ N. lat., 151° 27′ E. long. Lutke's chart.
Fahieu Oriental, 8° 30′ N. lat., 151° 23′ E. long. Spanish chart.
Namonuito or Anonima, north Islet, 9° 00′ N. lat., 150° 14′ E. long.; east Islet, 8° 34′ N. lat., 150° 32′ E. long., west Islet, 8° 35′ N. lat., 149° 47 E. long. Lutke's chart. (Triangular) S. E. point of triangle, 8° 30′ N. lat., 150° 35′ E. long.; S. W. do. 8° 32′ N. lat., 149° 49′ E. long.; N. do., 8° 58′ N. lat., 150° 19′ E. long. Spanish chart.
Tamatam or Martyr's Islands, S. Islet, 7° 32′ N. lat., 149° 29′ E. long. Duperrey's chart. Ollap, centre, 7° 35′ N. lat., 149° 27′ E. long. Spanish chart.
Poloat or Kata Island, centre, 7° 19½′ N. lat., 149° 17′ E. long. Freycinet in Findlay.
Palluot (two islands) 7° 20′ N. lat. 149° 14′ E. long. Spanish chart.
Luk or Ibargoita Island, centre, 6° 40′ N. lat., 149° 08′ E. long. Freycinet in Findlay. 6° 40′ N. lat., 149° 23′ E. long. Capt. Cheyne.
Pulu Suge, bank and island, centre, 6° 43′ N. lat., 149° 29′ E. long. Spanish chart.
Pikelot or Coquilla Island, centre, 8° 12′ N. lat., 147° 40′ E. long. Duperrey's chart.
Biguela Island, centre, 8° 12′ N. lat., 147° 39′ E. long. Spanish chart.
Pikela or Lydia Island, centre, 8° 38′ N. lat., 147° 13′ E. long. Duperrey's chart. Not on Spanish chart.
Satawal or Tucker's Island, centre, 7° 21′ N. lat., 147° 06′ E. long. Duperrey's chart.
Satahoal, centre, 7° 20′ N. lat., 147° 07′ E. long. Spanish chart.
Faiu (west), 8° 03′ N. lat., 146° 40′ E. long. Lutke's chart.
Fahieu Occidental reef, centre, 8° 02′ N. lat., 146° 49′ E. long. Spanish chart.
[Oraitillipou Bank] doubtful, between Pikelot and Faiu, west, eleven fathoms over it.
Lamotrek or Swede's Island, centre, 7° 29′ N. lat., 146° 28′ E. long. Lutke's chart.
Lamurrec, centre, 7° 30′ N. lat., 146° 29′ E. long. Spanish chart.

Elato or Haweis Island, N. point, 7° 29′ N. lat., 146° 19′ E. long. Lutke's chart.
Elato or Namoliaur Island, centre, 7° 28′ N. lat., 146° 19′ E. long. Spanish chart.
Olimario Islands, centre, 7° 43′ N. lat., 145° 57′ E. long. Lutke's chart. 7° 40′ N. lat., 145° 57′ E. long. Spanish chart.
Faraulep or Gardener's Island, centre, 8° 34′ N. lat., 144° 37′ E. long. Lutke's chart. Centre, 8° 48′ N. lat., 144° 36′ E. long. Spanish chart.
Ianthe Shoal, centre, 5° 53′ N. lat., 145° 39′ E. long. Capt. Cheyne. 6 feet water some parts.
Falipi Bank, centre, 5° 53′ N. lat., 145° 39′ E. long. Spanish chart.
Ifalik or Wilson's Island, centre, 7° 15′ N. lat., 144° 31′ E. long. Lutke's chart.
Ifeluc, centre, 7° 10′ N. lat., 144° 39′ E. long. Spanish chart.
Wolea or 13 Islands, E. point, 7° 21′ N. lat., 143° 58′ E. long. Lutke's chart. Entrance to lagoon, 7° 15′ N. lat., 144° 02′ E. long. Captain Cheyne.
Uleai, centre, 7° 20′ N. lat., 143° 56′ E. long. Spanish chart.
Eauripik or Kama Island, centre, 6° 39′ N. lat., 143° 11′ E. long. Lutke's chart.
Eurupig, centre, 6° 38′ N. lat., 143° 09′ E. long. Spanish chart.
Sorol or Philip Island, centre, 8° 06′ N. lat., 140° 52′ E. long. Lutke's chart.
Sorol Oriental Island, centre, 8° 05′ N. lat., 140° 49′ E. long. Spanish chart.
Fais or Tromlin's Island, centre, 9° 46′ N. lat., 140° 36′ E. long. Lutke's chart.
Feis Island, centre, 9° 45′ N. lat., 140° 37′ E. long. Spanish chart.
Uliti or McKenzie's Group, N. point of E. Group, 10° 06′ N. lat., 139° 47′ E. long.; Falalep, centre, 10° 02′ N. lat., 139° 50′ E. long.; S. point, 9° 47′ N. lat., 139° 42′ E. long. Lutke's chart. S. Islet, 9° 47′ N. lat., 139° 35′ E. long. D'Urville's chart.
Ulevi, W. group, centre, 10° 00′ N. lat., 139° 43′ E. long. Spanish chart.
Or Egoi, E. group, centre, 9° 50′ N. lat., 139° 59′ E. long. Spanish chart.
Hunter's Shoal, centre, 9° 57½′ N. lat., 138° 13′ E. long. In Findlay, 16 fathoms water on it. 9° 57′ N. lat., 138° 29′ E. long. Doubtful, in Spanish chart.
Eap, S. point, 9° 25′ N. lat., 138° 00′ E. long.; N. point, 9° 40′ N. lat., 138° 09′ E. long. D'Urville's chart.
Uyap, centre, 9° 30′ N. lat., 138° 09′ E. long. Spanish chart.
Ngoli or Lamoliork, S. Islet, 8° 17′ N. lat., 137° 33′ E. long.; N. E. Islot, 8° 35′ N. lat., 137° 40′ E. long. Captain Cheyne. Middle point, 8° 30′ N. lat., 137° 25′ E. long. D'Urville's chart.
Ulu or Lamoliaur, centre, 8° 20′ N. lat., 137° 34′ E. long. Spanish chart.
Palau, Pelew or Arecifos Islands, S. point, 6° 55′ N. lat., 134° 05′ E. long.; Angour Island, centre, 7° 35′ N. lat., 134° 30′ E. long. D'Urville's chart. Kyangle Island, 8° 08½′ N. lat., 134° 35′ E. long. Captain Cheyne. S. point of Pellelew Island, 6° 58′ N. lat., 134° 13′ E. long. Lieutenant Raper in Cheyne.
Babeldzuap or Pelew Islands and Reef, N. W. end of reef, 8° 40′ N. lat., 134° 09′; E. long.; Kianguel Island, centre, 8° 10′ N. lat., 134° 45′ E. long.; centre of west side of Babeldzuap, 7° 36′ N. lat., 134° 19′ E. long. Spanish chart. Babeldzuap, N. E. point, 7° 55′ N. lat., 134° 54′ E. long.; Angour Island, centre, 6° 51′ N. lat., 134° 14′ E. long.; Pelelew Island, S. point, 6° 58′ N. lat., 134° 24′ E. long., extensive reef from N. E. point Babeldzuap Islands, extending to N. W.
Sansoral or St. Andrew's Island, centre, 5° 20′ N. lat., 132° 16′ E. long. Horsburgh's Directory.
Sonrol, centre, 5° 19′ N. lat., 132° 14′ E. long. Spanish chart.
Codocopuey Island, 5° 15′ N. lat., 132° 14′ E. long. Spanish chart.
Matelotas, three islands, or Sequeras, centre, 8° 40′ North lat., 131° 34′ E. long. Spanish chart.

— 37 —

Pegan, centre, 0° 50′ N. lat., 134° 19′ E. long. Spanish chart.
Anna or Current Island, centre, 4° 39½′ N. lat., 132° 03½′ E. long. Horsburgh.
Anna or Pul Island, centre, 4° 38′ N. lat., 132° 09′ E. long. Spanish chart.
Merir or Warren Hastings' Island, centre, 4° 17½′ N. lat., 132° 28¼′ E. long. H. burgh.
Pulu Mariera Island, centre, 4° 12′ N. lat., 132° 27′ E. long. Spanish chart.
Tobi or Lord North's Island, centre, 3° 03′ N. lat., 131° 20′ E. long. Horsburgh.
Lord North's Island, centre, 3° 03′ N. lat., 131° 09′ E. long. Spanish chart.
Helen's Shoal, centre, 2° 50′ N. lat., 131° 41′ E. long. Horsburgh.
St. Felix or Carteret bank, centre, 2° 48′ N. lat., 131° 41′ E. long. Spanish chart.

POSITIONS SAILED OVER BUT NO TRACE OF LAND, ROCKS, OR SHOALS.

Parappa Rock, 21° 30′ N. lat., 161° 18′ W. long.
Malloons Island, 19° 20′ N. lat., 165° 21′ W. long.
Wilson Island, 19° 22′ N. lat., 166° 50′ W. long.
Shoal, 18° 28′ N. lat., 170° 30′ W. long.
Reef, 16° 38′ N. lat., 160° 53′ W. long.
Shoal, 14° 50′ N. lat., 170° 32′ W. long.
Shoal, 13° 30′ N. lat., 170° 30′ W. long.
Island, 13° 04′ N. lat., 168° 22′ W. long.
Island, 11° 28′ N. lat., 163° 53′ W. long.
Paltron Island, 10° 18′ N. lat., 165° 25′ W. long.
San Pedro Island, 11° 10′ N. lat., 179° 02′ W. long.
Island, 8° 20′ N. lat., 170° 00′ W. long.
Davis Island, 6° 38′ N. lat., 170° 05′ W. long.
Island, 6° 33′ N. lat., 166° 03′ W. long.
Barbera Island, 3° 42′ N. lat., 173° 06′ W. long.
Reef, 3° 55′ N. lat., 174° 32′ W. long.
Malcin Island, 2° 57′ N. lat., 172° 45′ W. lat.
Matthew Island, 2° 07′ N. lat., 173° 26′ W. long.
Decker Island, 23° 22′ N. lat., 162° 50′ E. long.
Deseirta, 20° 10′ N. lat., 165° 20′ E. long.
Deseirta, 23° 12′ N. lat., 160° 50′ E. long.
Lamira Island, 20° 10′ N. lat., 164° 09′ E. long.
Island, 20° 28′ N. lat., 166° 54′ E. long.
Island, 18° 57′ N. lat., 163° 30′ E. long.
Wake Reef, 17° 50′ N. lat., 173° 45′ E. long.
Island, 16° 02′ N. lat., 171° 38′ E. long.
Island, 17° 10′ N. lat., 176° 52′ E. long.
Island, 15° 02′ N. lat., 176° 26′ E. long.
Tarquin Island, 17° 00′ N. lat., 160° 01′ E. long.
Reef, 17° 15′ N. lat., 159° 17′ E. long.

POSITIONS NOT YET CERTAIN WHETHER EXISTING OR NOT.

Reef, 10° 04′ N. lat., 179° 21′ W. long.
Barber Island, 9° 00′ N. lat., 178° 00′ W. long.
Knox Island, 5° 58′ N. lat., 172° 00′ W. long.
Reef, 23° 45′ N. lat., 164° 00′ E. long.
Camira Island, 21° 32′ N. lat., 160° 00′ E. long.
Shoal, 18° 30′ N. lat., 173° 45′ E. long.
St. Bartholomew Island, 14° 40′ N. lat., 174° 25′ E. long.

FIRST PRINTING AT THE HAWAIIAN ISLANDS.

The first Printing Press at the Hawaiian Islands was imported by the American missionaries, and landed from the brig *Thaddeus*, at Honolulu, in April, 1820. It was not unlike the first used by Benjamin Franklin, and was set up in a thatched house standing a few fathoms from the old mission frame house, but was not put in operation until the afternoon of January 7, 1822.

At this inauguration there were present, his Excellency Governor Kiamoku (Kalanimoku), a chief of the first rank, with his retinue; some other chiefs and natives; Rev. Hiram Bingham, missionary; Mr. Loomis, printer (who had just completed setting it up); James Hunnewell; Captain William Henry and Captain Masters (Americans). Of these named, Mr. Bingham and Mr. Hunnewell are the only survivors [August, 1868]. Mr. Loomis "set up" Lesson I. of a spelling-book. Kiamoku (Kalanimoku) was instructed how to work the press, and struck off the first impression printed in the Hawaiian Islands. Mr. Loomis struck off the second, and Mr. Hunnewell the third. The last mentioned impression has been given by Mr. Hunnewell to the "American Board," and is now in the Mission collection, Pemberton Square, Boston. It is a sheet four by six inches, headed "Lesson I.," beneath which are twelve lines, each having five separate syllables of two letters. This was certainly the first printing at the Hawaiian Islands, and probably the first on the shores of the North Pacific Ocean. This account is from Mr. Hunnewell (who visited the island before the *Thaddeus*, in which vessel, also, he arrived with the press), and is transscribed from his personal explanations, and from his notes made at the time of the event described.

A MISSIONARY EPISODE.

Shortly after the arrival of the first missionaries at the Hawaiian Islands, a small party of them landed from a schooner at Hilo, on their way to visit the volcano of Kilauea. At that time no missionary had been stationed at Hilo, and consequently but few of the people of the place had ever had the opportunity of hearing preaching.

As the party were detained in the village over Sunday, they appointed morning and afternoon services. It so happened that the only building large enough for the proposed meetings was a canoe house situated on the beach. Thither the congregation assembled at the appointed time in the forenoon, filling the house to its utmost capacity. There were old scarred and white headed warriors, who had fought in the wars of Kamehameha, sitting in their *kapa kiheis*, through whose quiet dignity of manner there shone a certain expression of expectation; there were dried up old crones, to whom the emancipation from the *kapu* had come almost too late; and there were younger people and children and babies, more or less dressed, according to the convenience or whim or wealth of each individual. The posts which supported the roof of the house were appropriated by some of the more agile boys, to elevate themselves above the crowd, where, clinging on like monkeys, they awaited proceedings with countenances expressive of the greatest triumph and delight. Others, with equal ingenuity and greater comfort, climbed on to the outside of the roof, and by stealthily enlarging small holes, which they found through the thatch, or making new ones, had an unobstructed view of the inside, and the enormous size of their eyes, visible from below, showed how they appreciated it.

Under these favorable circumstances the meeting commenced, the preaching was listened to with great attention by the audience, and the missionaries felt that they were making an impression; suddenly, when the meeting was about half through, there ensued a scene of the wildest confusion; men and women rushed out of the building through the uncovered sides, or wherever there was an aperture large enough, rolling over each other in the attempt, and screaming most unaccountably; babies screeched as they were tossed around in the panic, little boys dropped from the posts and rolled from the roof. In less than a minute the house was empty, excepting the missionaries, and an immense hog which quietly made its bed on the straw on the middle of the floor. At the beginning of the disturbance, the missionaries supposed that it was a sudden attack from a hostile tribe, or an uprising against themselves; but they soon ascertained that the black hog which lay grunting in comfort on the straw, a "*puaa anaana*" (a six foot hog), as the natives call those of that size, belonged to Queen Kaahumanu, and was held sacred by the natives; that the canoe house was its accustomed resort in the heat of day, and its abrupt entrance among the crowd, swinging its sharp tusks from side to side with perfect contempt of the common people, was sufficient to cause the exodus described. In the afternoon the meeting was disturbed in the same manner.

There is no reliable authority that the missionaries made any satisfactory progress at Hilo till Kaahumanu's pig died.

THE HAWAIIAN VOLCANOES.

AN ERUPTION OF MAUNA LOA.

On Friday, March 28th, at 5.30 A. M., men on the whaleships anchored in Kawaihae harbor saw a dense pillar of smoke rise from the summit of Mauna Loa. The position of this smoke, and the bright reflection on its lower mass, showed the existence of fire in the terminal crater Mokuaweoweo. In a few hours, however, the smoke dispersed, and at night no light was seen. About 10 A. M., on the 28th, a slight shock of earthquake was felt in Kona and Kau, and in a few hours this was repeated, and again with decreasing intervals, and greater intensity, until at 1 P. M. a shock was felt "as if an immense boulder was hurled up under the foundations of our house." The shocks then were frequent and severe. The intervals between the distinct shocks did not average over three minutes until 11 P. M., when the intervals increased, and the violence of the disturbance abated about 1 P. M. on Sunday. The tremulous motion during this time was continuous, and stone walls, stone houses, and loose rocks on the *pali* above Kealakeakua Bay were thrown down. On Monday, Tuesday and Wednesday the motion continued with varying force. In Kau, on Wednesday at sunrise a severe shake was felt, and another at five, P. M.

Nearly all that night the shaking was very severe and frequent, accompanied by a rumbling sound from the earth. Up to this time no material damage had been done, although the people had abandoned their houses and taken to tents, as the cracking of the plastering and the constant noise of upsetting furniture, led them to fear some worse catastrophe. Between 4 and 5 p. m. on Thursday, April 2, an earthquake occurred which threw down every stone wall, and nearly every stone, frame or thatch house in Kau, doing much damage in Kona, Hilo, and other districts of Hawaii, while it was felt even on Kauai, some three hundred miles from Mauna Loa. In Honolulu clocks were stopped. In Kau the shock was most severe. Persons, and even horses, and other animals were thrown to the ground. Every church but one was destroyed; the walls of the large one at Waiohinu crumbled and the roof fell in— all the work of ten seconds. A gentleman riding on horseback found his horse lying flat under him before he could think of the cause, so sudden was the shock.

Mr. F. C. Lyman writes: " First the earth swayed to and fro north and south, then east and west, round and round, then up and down and in every imaginable direction for several minutes, everything crashing around us; the trees threshing about as if torn by a mighty rushing wind. It was impossible to stand; we had to sit on the ground, bracing with hands and feet, to keep from rolling over."

At this moment at Kapapala the sides of a mountain valley were rent by the shock, and the waters, probably drainings from the swamps several thousand feet above, were suddenly liberated, and so vast was the pressure that the contents of the subterranean reservoirs, water and sediment, were thrown with great force and velocity, the resulting mass reaching nearly two miles from the opening. Visitors report, that from the fissures to the commencement of the pile of mud ejected, stones are scattered in every direction for eighteen hundred feet; between the stones and the mud is a small clear space in which a native grass house is standing uninjured. The pile of mud or earth is from half a mile to a mile wide, two and a half miles long, and from two to thirty feet deep. As it poured through the valley it swept away and destroyed men, animals and trees. Thirty-one people and many hundred head of cattle were buried alive. The stream of water, at first muddy, and smelling strongly of clay and earth, after a few days became clear, and at last reports was still running a stream of sweet water.

From Thursday until Sunday the earth was in a constant commotion; people were made seasick, and strange noises were heard in the bowels of the earth. The most remarkable effect of the shock on Thursday was the agitation of the sea. Whether the shore line has been raised or depressed is not determined, but the shock drove the waves out, and on their return they swept far up on the land, carrying destruction. The height of this wave, which extended from Kaalualu harbor to Apua, a distance of fifty miles, varied at different places. At Waiohinu it was probably greatest, and reached forty feet. At Keauhou everything, even the stone houses, was swept away by the sea. At Hilo, although the shock was severe, the wave did not do much damage. The ground was much cracked, some of the rents extending many rods. No damage was done to the north side of the island beyond the detaching of loose stones from the cliffs. On Friday a shock was felt more severely on Oahu than on Hawaii.

On Tuesday, April 7th, lava burst forth in Kau above Kahuku, through an enormous fissure three miles long, which seems to have opened without any remarkable commotion. The lava ran in a few hours (no one noted the exact time, as the neighborhood was enveloped in smoke) over a distance of twelve miles, from a height, according to Dr. Hillebrand, of 3,800 feet, to the sea, extending the coast line more than half a mile. This eruption ceased either on Saturday or Sunday night, April 11th or 12th. Smoke was thrown into the air far above the trade wind, which was blowing strongly until Saturday, and carried over Oahu and Kauai, some three hundred miles. Vessels near by were sprinkled with ashes.

The lava welled up from the entire length of the crack simultaneously, and was not very abundant.

ERUPTION OF KILAUEA.

On Saturday, March 28th, there were frequent shocks of earthquake. Portions of the southwest cliff were shaken down, and the lakes of lava seemed quite active. Kaina, the owner of the Volcano House, had resided there for five months previously, and he reports that from January 20th to March 27th, "the crater had been unusually active; eight lakes being in constant ebullition, and frequently overflowing. During all this time there was in the northwest corner a blowhole, from which at regular intervals of a minute or less, large volumes of vapor were blown with a roaring noise, as from a steam engine." This ceased about the 17th of March, and at the same time the activity of the lakes was greatly increased. March 27th the first shock was felt, and two days later the bottom of the crater was overflowed and incandescent.

On April 2d the great shock of earthquake caused the whole vicinity of the crater to rock like a ship at sea. "At that moment there commenced fearful detonations in the crater; large quantities of lava were thrown up to a great height, and portions of the wall tumbled in. This extraordinary commotion, accompanied with an unearthly noise and ceaseless swaying of the ground, continued from that day until Sunday night, April 5th; but from the first the fire began to recede. On Thursday night it was already confined to the regular lakes; on Saturday night it only remained in the great south lake (Halemaumau), and on Sunday night there was none at all." Fire has since reappeared in this dwelling of Pele. The lava also appeared in one of the lateral craters east of Kilauea on April 2d, but whether in Poliokeawe or in Kilaueaiki, it is impossible to determine, the names are so confused in the various reports. At Kapapala, however, near the site of the eruption of Kilauea in 1823, a crack has opened and lava has oozed out, but by no means in sufficient quantity to lead to the supposition that this is the conduit by which Kilauea has empted itself.

Dr. Hillebrand describes the present condition of this crater as follows: "The ground about the crater, particularly on the eastern and western sides, is rent by a great number of fissures, one near the Puna road more than twelve feet wide and very deep; others of less size run parallel to and cross the Kau road so as to render travel on it very dangerous. The lookout house is detached from the main land by a very deep *crevasse*, and stands now on an isolated, overhanging rock, which, at the next severe concussion, must tumble into the pit below. Many smaller fissures are hidden by grass and bushes, forming so many traps for the unwary. The Volcano House, however, has not suffered, nor is the ground surrounding it broken in the least. From the walls of Kilauea large masses of rock have been detached and thrown down. On the west and northwest side, where the fire had been most active before the great earthquake of April 2d, the falling masses probably have been at once melted by the lava and carried off in its stream, for the walls there remain as perpendicular as they were before; but that this part of the wall has lost portions of its mass, is shown too evidently by the deep crevices along the western edge just spoken of, and the partial detachment in many. places of large prisms of rock. But it is on the east and northeast particularly that the character of the wall has undergone a change. Along the descent in the second ledge large masses of rock, many, more than one hundred tons in weight, obstruct the path and form abutments to the stone pillars,—small buttress hills similar to those observed in front of the high basaltic wall in Koolau, Oahu. So, also, in the deep crater itself, the eastern wall has lost much of its perpendicular dip, and has become shelving in part. The great south lake (Halemaumau) is transformed into a vast pit more than five hundred feet deep, the solid eastern wall projecting far over the hollow below, while the remaining sides are falling off with a sharp inclination, and consist of a confused mass of clinkers. More than two thirds of the old floor of Kilauea has caved in, and sunk from one to three hundred feet below the level of the remaining floor. The depression embraces the whole western half, and infringes in a semicircular line on a considerable portion of the other half. It is deepest in the northern and slopes gradually to the southern end."

This is the first time since 1840 that Kilauea has emptied its great crater to such an extent, and this eruption is also the first since 1832, when both Kilauea and Mauna Loa have been in simultaneous eruption. The crater of Mokuaweoweo, on Mauna Loa, has been very active twice since 1865, but no lava has run out, and no one has ascended the mountain, as the outbreaks occurred in winter, when the snows make the ascent more difficult and even dangerous.

The earthquake shocks have been comparatively superficial, as is shown by their very circumscribed area, and are perhaps due to the very great rainfall which has penetrated the porous and fissured dome to the central fires which were on the point of breaking out. In other words, the eruption of Mauna Loa would have taken place soon, had no drop of rain fallen on Hawaii; but its advent would have been quiet as usual,—no shocks, a simple parting of the mountain walls in the weakest place, and a gushing torrent of lava. The earthquakes seem to have been caused in great part by the water reaching the net-work of hot material which was gradually penetrating the fissures of the mountain, and the explosive shocks resulted. The violence of these may have caused a premature tapping of the lava reservoirs of Mauna Loa as well as those of Kilauea, and this is made more probable by the unusually small quantity of lava ejected.

There seems to be some doubt whether the outbreak at Kahuku came from Mauna Loa or Kilauea; but if Dr. Hillebrand gives the correct elevation of this crack, it must have been above the lava in Kilauea as well as forty miles distant. It is much to be hoped that some scientific man may be sent out to examine carefully the effects of this whole volcanic disturbance, as it presents an opportunity to solve several difficult problems which have long engaged the attention of seismic geologists.

THE HAWAIIAN FLORA.

From the time of Captain Cook's visit to the Hawaiian Islands, the vegetable productions of this group have attracted the interest of botanists, but it was not until last year that any comprehensive elaboration of the Flora appeared. Mr. Horace Mann, in his "Enumeration of Hawaiian Plants," has supplied the want, and greatly increased the interest in the unique Flora. From this work most of the following details have been gathered.

Of the botanists who have visited the Islands, Menzies, Chamisso, Gaudichaud, Macrae, Douglas, Brackenridge, Pickering and Remy, made the largest collections, and their specimens are in various European herbaria. Dr. Wm. Hillebrand of Honolulu has recently sent many interesting contributions to Kew and to Mr. Mann. But by far the largest collection ever made was that of Mr. Mann and his companion in 1864–5. Various statistics of this series are given below, so far as they relate to the flowering plants. The grasses have not yet been published; the ferns, including Lycopodiaceæ, as at present determined, number thirty genera and one hundred and thirty-four species; and the lichens forty-two genera and one hundred and thirty species.

| | Genera. | Species. | Endemic. | | Genera of Endemic Species only. | Families of Endemic Species only. | Aboriginal? | Introduced Species. | New Genera. | New Species. |
			Genera.	Species.				Recent.		
Amaranthaceæ	5	9	2	3						
Anacardiaceæ	1	1								
Apocynaceæ	4	5	4		3			1		1
Araliaceæ	6	7	3	7	2	*			1	2
Aroideæ	2	2								
Basellaceæ	1	1					1			
Begoniaceæ	1	1	1	1		*				
Bixaceæ	1	1		1	1	*				
Borraginaceæ	3	4						1		
Capparidaceæ	2	2								
Caryophyllaceæ	3	14	2	14	1	*			1	6
Celastraceæ	1	1		1	1					
Chenopodiaceæ	2	5		1						
Commelynaceæ	2	2						2		
Compositæ	24	59	6	46	5			10	1	4
Convolvulaceæ	6	13		8	3		1			
Cruciferæ	3	4		2	1			2		1
Curcubitaceæ	3	6	1	4			2			1
Cyperaceæ	14	40	2	22	6			1		4
Dioscoreaceæ	2	2					2			
Droseraceæ	1	1								
Ebenaceæ	1	2		2	1	*				
Epacridæ	1	2								
Ericaceæ	1	2		2	1	*				
Euphorbiaceæ	7	14		8	2		2	3		1
Gentianaceæ	1	1		1	1	*				
Geraniaceæ	2	6		4	1			2		
Gesneriaceæ	1	14		14	1	*				4
Goodeniaceæ	1	6		5	1					
Guttiferæ	1	1					1			
Halorageæ	1	1		1	1	*				
Hydrophyllaceæ	1	1		1	1	*				
Ilicinæ	1	1	1	1		*				1
Iridaceæ	1	1		1	1					
Juncaceæ	2	2		1						
Labiatæ	4	29	2	28	1					4
Lauraceæ	2	2		1	1					1
Leguminosæ	19	29		11	5		8	4		1
Liliaceæ	4	5		3	2					
Lobeliaceæ	6	35	5	35	1	*			1	10
Loganiaceæ	1	5	1	5		*				3
Loranthaceæ	1	1								
Lythraceæ	2	2						1		
Malvaceæ	6	16		10				3		1
Menispermaceæ	2	3		1						
Myoporineæ	1	1	1	1		*				
Myrsinaceæ	1	3		3	1	*				
Myrtaceæ	3	6		2			1	1		
Naidaceæ	3	5								
Nyctaginaceæ	2	3								
Oleaceæ	1	1		1	1	*				
Onagraceæ	1	1					1			
Orchidaceæ	2	3	1	3	1					1
Palmeæ	2	4	1	3	1					1
Pandanaceæ	2	2		1	1					
Papayaceæ	1	1					1			
Phytolaccaceæ	1	1					1			
Piperaceæ	2	13		8	1					3
Pittosporaceæ	1	6		6	1	*				
Plantaginaceæ	1	3		2				1		
Plumbaginaceæ	1	1								

	Genera.	Species.	Genera.	Endemic Species.	Genera of Endemic Species only.	Families of Endemic Species only.	Aboriginal?	Introduced Species. Recent.	New Genera.	New Species.
Polygonaceæ	2	3		1				1		
Portulaccaceæ	2	3		2	1					
Primulaceæ	1	2								
Ranunculaceæ	1	2		2	1	*				
Rhamnaceæ	3	7		5	1					
Rosaceæ	4	5	1	4	3					
Rubiaceæ	18	33	3	28	5		1	1		5
Rutaceæ	4	17	2	17	2	*			1	6
Santalaceæ	2	3		3	2					
Sapindaceæ	2	3					1			
Sapotaceæ	1	1		1	1	*				
Saxifragaceæ	1	1		1	1	*				
Scrophulariaceæ	2	2						1		
Smilacinæ	1	3		3						1
Solanaceæ	4	12	1	9	1		1	1		1
Sterculiaceæ	2	3		1		-	1	1		
Taccaceæ	1	1								
Ternstrœmiaceæ	1	1		1	1	*				
Thymelaceæ	1	6		5						
Tiliaceæ	1	1		1	1	*				
Umbelliferæ	3	3		1	1			1		
Urticaceæ	11	14	2	8	4		2			
Verbenaceæ	4	4						3		
Violaceæ	2	6	1	6	1	*				1
Zinziberaceæ	2	2						1		
Zygophyllaceæ	1	1								
	253	553	39	373	76	26	27	42	5	71

Taking all the plants both native and introduced, we have as the proportion of species to each genus, ... 2.58
The endemic genera alone, ... 3.94
The genera represented only by endemic species, ... 1.28
Introduced genera, ... 1.07
Endemic genera of only one species, ... 16
Genera of a single endemic species, ... 49
Introduced genera of one species, ... 43
Other genera of one species, ... 45
Percentage of all the endemic species, ... 67.4
    " species of endemic genera, ... 28.
    " introduced species, ... 10.7
    " species discovered by Mann and Brigham, ... 11.4
    " species found elsewhere, ... 10.5

In the first column are given the names of the families of plants; in the second and third the genera and species; then the endemic genera and species; the genera and families represented only by peculiar species; the introduced species of which our knowledge is mostly conjectural in one column, those known to be of recent introduction in the next; and finally the new genera and species first made known by Mr. Mann's collection. In the genera are included the six subgenera, Sicyocarya, Pterotropia, Campylotheca, Raillardia, Polycœlium and Nototrichium. The coconut, pandanus, cordyline *(ki)*, bread-fruit and kalo, are here regarded as indigenous, as the first settlers must have had something to live on, and there is no evidence of their introduction other than the fact that they are most abundant near settlements. It is probable that one species of banana is native, but these are at present but little known.

The new genera of flowering plants described by Mr. Mann, are Alsinidendron, H. Mann; Platydesma, H. Mann; Dipanax, Seeman; Hesperomannia, A. Gray; Brighamia, A. Gray.

Many of the introduced species have become completely natualized, as the verbena *(oi)* and indigo, and, like the introduced plants on St. Helena, have in many cases driven off the native vegetation. Remy endeavored to divide the island flora into five regions, but with little success. The shore zone is where most of the introduced plants are found, and is usually arid, sandy or rocky, and produces no luxuriant vegetation, but the plants are by no means exclusively littoral, or submaritime. The valleys have been so long the dwelling of man, and have been cultivated and cleared to such an extent that they are not at all distinct; where they are well watered they are quite tropical. Above the height of eight hundred to a thousand feet the mountains are densely wooded on the windward side, and the limit of vegetation is determined by the aspect; on the windward side of Mauna Kea it reaches to a height of nearly twelve thousand feet, while on the lee of Mauna Loa it ceases at eight thousand feet. There is no truly alpine zone, the trees and shrubs of the lower regions become stunted, and finally disappear, and the upper regions are quite destitute of vegetable life.

THE natives in Kona, Hawaii, have recently raised a new bell upon a neat tower which they have erected, attached to one of their churches. It was heard tolling for a long time, and when inquiry was made, the good people replied that they were about burying, in a becoming manner, some old conch shells, which had been blown for assembling the people to church during the past forty-eight years, and it appeared proper to strike the bell forty-eight times!—*Friend.*

REV. ASA THURSTON.

On the eleventh of last March, this venerable missionary died in Honolulu. We quote from the Pacific Commercial Advertiser of the fourteenth of the same month.

"Rev. Asa Thurston was born at Fitchburg, Mass., Oct. 12th, 1787, and died in Honolulu, March 11th, 1868, at the advanced age of eighty years. He graduated at Yale College, in New Haven, in 1816, and at Andover Theological Seminary in 1819. Among his classmates at Andover were his associate, the Rev. Hiram Bingham; the Rev. Cyrus Byington, missionary to the Choctaws; the Rev. Dr. King, missionary to Athens, Greece, and several others who have become distinguished for their talents as divines or scholars. Soon after leaving the Seminary he was married to Miss Lucy Goodale of Marlborough, Mass., who has ever been his faithful wife and companion in all the toils, labors and privations of missionary life. They embarked at Boston, Oct. 23d, 1819, with their associates, on board the brig Thaddeus, Capt. Blanchard. Before sailing, Mr. Thurston made a farewell address in Park Street Church. The vessel reached the Islands March 30th, 1820, and Mr. and Mrs. Thurston were assigned to the station at Kailua, Hawaii, the old residence of Hawaiian kings. There they resided for more than forty years, until, through the infirmities of age, they removed to Honolulu. Here he spent the few closing years of an eventful life, respected, honored and beloved. As a missionary of the American Board, he has ever labored with great usefulness and success. His knowledge of the native language and character was most thorough. As a preacher he was ever popular among the Hawaiians, as he spoke their language with great purity and idiomatic accuracy. In the early years of the mission, his labors as a translator were arduous and successful. In this great work it fell to his lot to translate parts of Genesis, Numbers, Deuteronomy, and the whole of Samuel, 2d of Kings, and some other parts of the Bible.

"His funeral was attended on Thursday last, by both Hawaiians and foreigners, from the First Church in Honolulu."

It falls to the lot of but few men to witness such great changes as he has witnessed, the result in great measure of his own efforts;

or to reap on earth such a glorious reward for a life-long work as he enjoyed ere he passed away. When the brig Thaddeus anchored on the shores of Hawaii, the members of this Christian "Forlorn Hope," Capt. Hunnewell, who was an officer on the brig, tells us, were filled with the deepest anxiety as to what reception the chiefs and people would give them, fearing, even, lest they should not be allowed to land at all as teachers. Great, then, was their astonishment when they learned that a revolution had in a few months performed for them the work of years; that the people had destroyed their idols, had desecrated their temples, and had, with almost universal consent, broken up the most binding religious laws, which, with all the authority of ancient custom, and strengthened by a most vivid superstitious belief, had held them in servitude for ages; that a nation of skeptics, believing in nothing, despising the past, and by the teachings of their own prophets, waiting and hoping for a new and better light from beyond the seas, were ready to give them an enthusiastic welcome as the apostles of a new civilization. Such was Mr. Thurston's first experience in missionary life. His few last years, after forty years of toil, were spent among his friends, and in the midst of the people he had helped to civilize; years of quiet and well earned rest. And as we saw him at church, or met him on the street, his venerable figure, with his hoary head and flowing beard, was ever to us the fulfilment of our ideal of the old patriarchs of Bible times.

JOHN P. PARKER.

MR. JOHN P. PARKER died at Honolulu, March 25, 1868, at the advanced age of seventy-eight. He was born at Newton, Massachusetts, and at the age of seventeen commenced a seafaring life on a vessel trading with the Northwest Coast and China. After touching at the Hawaiian Islands several times, he finally decided to settle on Hawaii about the year 1815, and was in the service of Kamehameha I., who fully appreciated his integrity and worth. After the death of this king, in 1819, Mr. Parker lived at Waiapuka, in the rich, well-watered district of North Kohala, and here this pioneer acquired a great reputation among the natives by his skill in fishing and in hunting wild cattle among the mountains; he was indeed the first one allowed to use his gun on the cattle introduced by Vancouver, which had been under a strict *kapu*.

About the year 1835 he removed to Waimea, first building up the place now known as Puuloa, and about ten years afterwards, the ranch at Mana in Hamakua. Here for the past quarter of a century he lived, surrounded by his children and many assistants, and fully occupied with his immense herds of cattle and sheep. Here, too, the traveller always found a hearty welcome, and no one would care to go from Kawaihae to Hilo without making Mr. Parker's house a station for at least one night. We well remember one dark night, when belated and lost on a sorry beast, we heard the dogs barking, and soon saw lights, and before we had time to look about, we were welcomed by the venerable host, and seated at a grand koa table, forgetting the long weary ride and the wretched nag. Then he would tell us his stories of the olden time on Hawaii, and we would see the tusks of the wild boars he and his sons had killed, and in the cool, bright morning, he would show us his splendid horses, the best on Hawaii, and all the while he was surrounded by his grandchildren and a band of natives who evidently regarded him as the patriarch of the region. The Hawaiians always loved him, and he took a wife from their number, with whom he lived happily forty years, until her death. Some six months before his death he made profession of his Christian faith, and was baptized by the two missionaries of his neighborhood, for whom he had always shown great respect. He may have forgotten the many who received his hospitality, but these friends, now scattered all over the world, will ever remember the Patriarch of Hawaii.

The Rev. S. C. Damon, D. D., preached the funeral discourse at the Bethel on the Sunday following his decease, and his remains were conveyed to Hawaii, to rest beside those of his wife, son and daughter. He leaves one son, several grandchildren and two great grandchildren.

CURRENT EVENTS.

Perhaps never before in Hawaiian history has the nation been so distinctly divided into two political parties. The feeling of political discontent has been steadily increasing, and this feeling is daily assuming a more active and offensive attitude. The Liberal party is growing larger and stronger. The February elections were attended with considerable excitement and party bitterness. The Opposition fiercely accused the other party with tampering with the rights of voters at the polls, and published considerable evidence to that effect. There was also talk of challenging the rights of certain members to sit in the House on the ground of illegal election; but nothing was done, and, whether the charges were with or without foundation, it is probable that the stir that was made will have a beneficial effect on future elections. The Opposition elected a majority to the House. The Legislature has met, performed its business and adjourned with a praiseworthy degree of promptness. The Opposition did not seem to have any systematic plan before them, and lost half their strength for want of concerted action. A subsidy bill was passed, against the wishes of many liberal members, to aid the California line of steamers to the amount of twenty-five thousand dollars a year. It may be a good investment in the end. The request of the King to have his salary raised was granted with little opposition, and forty-five thousand dollars a year voted for his support. A bill was passed taxing horses of an inferior grade much less than before, while the tax on the better class remains the same. This seems impolitic, as it is a premium on bad horses, which are altogether too numerous on the Islands. Since the first horses were landed in 1803, the breed has not been carefully improved, and the fact that a bad horse costs as much to keep as a good one has been lost sight of.

War received its usual large appropriation, far beyond what was voted for educational purposes. It is strange how quietly this large item of army expenses is acquiesced in by the people; it is a costly humbug—they receive nothing in return but feathers, parades and salutes of blank cartridges from "Brown Bess" muskets.

An attempt was made during the session to bring Mr. Whitney, the editor of the "Pacific Commercial Advertiser," before the House on the charge of publishing traitorous articles, but it ended as it commenced, in talk.

The Reciprocity Treaty has been tabled by its friends, because a two-thirds vote could not be obtained. Minister Harris has labored faithfully and constantly, and his present failure is much to be regretted. The Hawaiian Club has done much to help him, spending money and time in their efforts to advance free trade between the two countries. Unfortunately the question of annexation impeded the negotiation, both here and at the Islands, and many who wished the Islands well considered the proposed treaty as made mainly in favor of the California sugar refiners.

So much has lately been said about annexation of the Hawaiian Kingdom to the United States, that the subject cannot be wholly passed by here. Annexation has never been the policy of the United States. Annexationists in the present case have a great deal to say about the importance of American interests at the Islands, and the great advantage to both countries if they had one flag and one government. We believe that no one has a better knowledge of the importance of the United States to the Islands than the Hawaiians themselves, and we regard the interests of the natives as paramount, and any interests that interfere with them or override them as illegal and inimical. Under the present attitude of the two governments there could be no annexation except by force, and there seems to be nothing in the situation which would authorize or excuse such a procedure.

King Kamehameha V. is reported to have said, in view of the increasing American influence at the Islands, that, if the Americans did not let him alone, he would hoist the British flag, and put himself under British protection; which would give the annexationists the *casus belli* they desire.

The record of the stay of the U. S. S. *Lackawanna* at the Islands is a strange one. Sent at the request of one of the Hawaiian Government ministers, the instructions to her officers were liberal and generous in the extreme, and, so far as we can learn, the conduct of her commander, a well-known friend to Hawaiian interests, and her officers, was what was to be expected of their position. While cruising round the group, the *Lackawanna* rescued a ship's company that had been wrecked on one of the barren reefs several hundred miles to the northward; several of these shipwrecked persons were native Hawaiians. The Lieutenant-Governor of Hawaii, under instructions from the Minister of the Interior at Honolulu, refused the non-commissioned officers and crew permission to land at Hilo, an act of discourtesy to a friendly power unprecedented at the Islands. The indignation caused by this act, whether intended or not, was very damaging to the prospects of the Reciprocity Treaty. The excuse for this unfriendly act was the alleged misconduct of some of the crew while on an excursion to Puuloa, a small fishing village a few miles from Honolulu; we have no evidence of the truth of this charge except that given by the Minister of the Interior.

The demand of the Hawaiian Government for the removal of the *Lackawanna*, and the reply of the United States Government, would be interesting in this connection, and would throw much light on some dark things; but it has not been published, in deference, we understand, to the wishes of the Hawaiian Administration. The *Lackawanna* completed her cruise, and was relieved some months ago by the U. S. S. *Mohongo*.

We rejoice to see that measures have been taken to secure a lighthouse at the entrance to Honolulu Harbor, a much needed public improvement. His Majesty's Government could not erect a more desirable monument. We well remember our arrival after dark off Honolulu, and the expense we were put to in burning a quart of turpentine as a signal, all unnoticed, and we were obliged to patiently wait for the Pele next morning.

Among the internal improvements proposed by the Legislature, the attempt to improve inter-island steam navigation perhaps ranks first. Thirty thousand dollars were appropriated for the next two years, and the bill provides for the termination of the charter of the present company in six months from its passage, and the service will then be open to competition. It provides for one steamer to run to and around Hawaii, making this trip in one week, for two-thirds of the subsidy. The bill also provides for a steamer to run to Kauai, touching at every port, and making the circuit of that island once a week for five thousand dollars a year.

One hundred and forty-eight Japanese laborers arrived on the 18th of June. Six were accompanied by their wives. Their wages are fixed by contract at four dollars per month, with food, clothing, medical attendance, and free passage at the end of three years to Japan. Besides being more intelligent than the Chinese coolies hitherto imported, they appear healthier, and are more docile.

The vacancy on the Supreme Bench occasioned by the death of Judge Robertson, has been filled by the appointment of Gen. A. S. Hartwell to the position. The General is a Massachusetts man, and a graduate of Harvard College and Law School. During the war he served as Colonel of one of the Massachusetts colored regiments, and in other situations of responsibility, and near its close was breveted Brigadier.

A reception was given by the Hawaiian Club a few weeks ago in honor of Gen. Hartwell, at the residence of Gen. Marshall at Riverside ; at which were assembled the friends of the Club, old Island residents, and people interested in the Islands to the number of forty or fifty. The day was a perfect one, and with the pleasant meetings of acquaintances, the interchange of news and opinions, the spread of good things under the trees, together with croquet, boating, etc., all heightened by the friendly informality which characterizes the Club reunions, the afternoon passed only too quickly away. Gen. Hartwell sailed for the Islands the middle of August: the best wishes of his friends for his success go with him.

J. W. Austin, Esq., has also been appointed to the Supreme Bench, in place of Judge Davis, resigned.

It were pleasant to step out of the mud of politics for a little season, did not the next step launch us into a chaos of spouting lava, earthquakes, heavy surf, smoke, bad gases, and rivers of thick mud ; a combination worse than any two of Pharaoh's plagues. The earthquake and eruption which took place on Hawaii, at about the first of last April, was one of the great events of the century: and geologists, as they learn more about it, are disposed to regard it as one of the greatest earthquakes on record the world over. About a hundred people were killed; and the amount of property that was destroyed was very great. Contributions of money and clothes were made from different parts of the Islands for the sufferers, in which good work Queen Emma was very active. The King also did much to help them with gifts of clothes and the cheering influence of his presence and sympathy. It seems most desirable that a scientific expedition should be organized to explore the scene of the earthquake and eruption.

It is with peculiar feelings that we chronicle the loss of the schooner *Excel*, or *Moi wahine*, as she was more familiarly known. She was no ordinary craft, and was so old, years ago, that we never found any one who knew where she was built, or when. Before her advent at the Islands fifteen or twenty years ago, she did good service as a fishing smack on the Banks of Newfoundland. Of her history previous to that time we have no knowledge. At the time of her loss she was not the same vessel that she was when she first arrived. It is perhaps safe to say that she has been rebuilt half a dozen times. For the last ten years she has been in a chronic state of leakiness, and often when we have been compelled to take passage in her, we have wished that, ere we should have occasion to risk our valuable lives in her sugar-packed hull again, she might gently shiver her timbers against some friendly rock-bound coast, and decay where the winds and waves would ever chant over her a fitting requiem; but she was doomed to a more cruel fate. Blown out to sea from a shelterless guano island she has never since been heard from. She was a fair sailer, a capital sea-boat, and led a career of honor and usefulness.

Two of the American missionaries have died within the last year: Rev. Asa Thurston, one of the pioneers, who landed at the Islands in the year 1820; and Rev. E. Johnson of Kauai, who was sent as delegate to the Micronesian Missions, and died on the *Morning Star* just before reaching the island of Ebon, where he was buried. We also record the death of two old and well-known residents; Capt. B. F. Snow of Honolulu, and Mr. Parker, the patriarch of Hawaii.

We have lately had the pleasure of examining specimen copies of the revised edition of the Hawaiian Bible; it is published in octavo form for common use, and with wide margins as a quarto for the pulpit. The type is distinct, the paper clear, and the pages beautifully printed: there are full marginal references to both Old and New Testaments. As a translation, its improvement on the old edition is plainly noticeable; mistakes are corrected, and the language in places is more idiomatic. Mr. Clark, formerly of Honolulu, has had the supervision of the publishing of the work. It was printed at the New York Bible House. We congratulate the Hawaiian public on the acquisition of so perfect a Bible.

Another publication on the Hawaiian Islands has just come out; we refer to a translation of Jules Remy's "Tales of a Venerable Savage," by William T. Brigham, Esq., of Boston. Parts of the work have been translated before, and printed in the Honolulu papers, but it has never been published in a compact form. We find the translation to be very literal, and the style is easy and pleasant to the reader. It is published in a pamphlet form, and bears on the title-page a unique vignette, which is a faithful representation of Kamehameha's old war idol, now in the cabinet of Oahu College. Historically, and as throwing light on Hawaiian customs, the work is most valuable, and Mr. Brigham deserves the thanks of the public for the undertaking. As only two hundred copies were printed, copies are now comparatively scarce.

We have watched with interest the advent of a new public journal at Honolulu, the "Maile Quarterly." As its name denotes, it is published once a quarter, and is devoted to religion, literature and education, and to social and political questions pertaining to the Pacific Islands. There is a place in the literature of the Islands which needs to be filled by just such a periodical as this in its prospectus proposes to be; and the opportunity which the publishers of the Maile Quarterly have for making it a necessity, and gaining for it a wide and permanent influence, is too good to be lost.

Mr. Horace Mann's valuable "Enumeration of Hawaiian Plants" is soon to be followed by a complete Flora of the Islands, so that the people of Hawaii will have no excuse for any ignorance of the wonders of the vegetable world around them.

CUSTOM HOUSE STATISTICS—HAWAIIAN ISLANDS, 1867.

PREPARED BY W. F. ALLEN, COLLECTOR-GENERAL OF CUSTOMS.

IMPORTS---Port of Honolulu, Hawaiian Islands, 1867.

	VALUE GOODS PAYING DUTY	VALUE GOODS IN BOND.	TOTAL.
Ale, Porter and Beer,	$24,800 36	$8,725 82	$33,526 18
Animals,	204 00		204 00
Building Materials,	18,753 01		18,753 01
Clothing, Hats, Boots,	238,413 62	19,489 61	257,903 23
Crockery and Glassware,	8,131 46		8,131 46
Drugs,	19,074 95		19,074 95
Dry Goods, { Cottons,	229,260 27	12,883 83	242,144 10
Linens,	25,200 62		25,200 62
Silks,	14,508 82	888 88	15,397 70
Woolens,	84,228 00	7,709 62	91,937 62
Fancy Goods, Millinery, etc.,	44,704 46	3,101 15	47,805 61
Fish (dry and salt),	30,594 75		30,594 75
Flour,	24,704 18	21,529 82	46,234 00
Fruits (fresh),	2,699 46	26 00	2,725 46
Furniture,	18,436 42	197 02	18,633 44
Furs and Ivory,		23,178 00	23,178 00
Grain,	6,383 39	189 44	6,572 83
Groceries and Provisions,	59,718 66	86,855 00	146,573 66
Hardware, Agricultural Implements, Tools, etc.,	100,521 94	2,032 43	102,544 37
Iron and Steel,	8,836 41	7,726 28	16,562 69
Jewelry, Plate, Clocks,	11,692 52		11,692 52
Lumber,	57,586 70	45 00	57,631 70
Machinery,	3,842 89		3,842 89
Naval Stores,	35,845 94	57,875 84	93,721 78
Oils (whale, kerosene, cocoanut, etc.),	11,807 97	98,410 36	110,218 33
Opium,	7,776 90	7,153 00	14,929 90
Perfumery, Toilet Articles,	3,192 86	621 48	3,814 34
Paints and Paint Oils,	16,987 31	639 29	17,626 60
Saddlery, Carriages, etc.,	37,419 06	4,167 98	41,587 04
Shooks, Containers,	28,374 31	26,312 03	54,686 34
Spirits,		23,288 76	23,288 76
Stationery, Books, etc.,	26,010 93	522 51	26,533 44
Tea,	8,870 71	41 09	8,911 80
Tin, Tinware,	3,707 28		3,707 28
Tobacco, Segars,	28,659 66	22,346 55	51,006 21
Whalebone,		125,383 14	125,383 14
Wines (light),	6,726 65	1,724 72	8,451 37
Sundry merchandise, not included in the above,	25,443 36	15,537 07	40,980 43
Sundry merchandise imported by Whalers,	3,549 21		3,549 21
Sundry unspecified merchandise,	1,563 40	585 60	2,149 00
Charges on Invoices,	23,309 09	3,463 55	26,772 64
25 per cent. added on uncertified Invoices,	15,001 04		
	$1,316,542 57	$582,650 87	$1,899,193 44
Discounts,		$4,933 63	
Discounts on United States Currency,		54,930 61	
Damaged and Short,		3,520 57	
			63,384 81
			$1,835,808 63

Domestic Exports, Port of Honolulu, 1867.

Sugar, lbs.,	17,127,187
Molasses, galls.,	544,994
Paddy, lbs.,	572,099
Rice, lbs.,	441,750
Coffee, lbs.,	127,546
Salt, tons,	107
Fungus, lbs.,	167,666
Poi, bbls.,	649
Bananas, bchs.,	2,913
Cotton, lbs.,	13,512
Goat Skins, pcs.,	51,889
Hides, lbs.,	304,095
Tallow, lbs.,	60,939
Pulu, lbs.,	203,958
Wool, lbs.,	409,471
Whale Oil, galls.,	70,646
Sperm Oil, galls.,	58
Whalebone, lbs.,	48,444
Peanuts, lbs.,	16,315
Oranges, pkgs., 105 and	3,000
Limes, pkgs., 17 and	29,500
Cocoanuts,	20,265
Potatoes, bbls.,	221
Arrow-root, pkgs., 2 and lbs.,	325
Horns, pcs.,	19,225
Bones, lbs.,	127,904
Pumpkins,	450
Soap, lbs.,	250
Sandal Wood, pcs., 24 and lbs.,	5,463
Plants, pkgs.,	4
Beche le mer, lbs.,	4,958
Kukui Nuts, lbs.,	130
Ivory, lbs.,	1,702
Hay, bdls.,	35
Vegetables, kegs,	71
Gold Fish,	400
Oil Presses,	2
Rice Mills,	1
Shark Fins, cs.,	1
Horses,	12
Mules,	5
Bullock,	1
Sheep,	12
Curiosities, etc.,	

Total Value Domestic Produce, Including the Catch of Hawaiian Whalers, rates taken at Custom House, viz. :

Sperm oil $1 05 per gall., Whale oil 34 c. per gall., Coast oil 31 c. per gall., Arctic bone 62 c. per lb., Ochotsk bone 59 c. per lb., Kodiac bone 57 c. per lb., ...	$1,205,622 02
Furnished as Supplies to Whalers, as per estimate, . . .	72,100 00
" " Merchantmen, ...	26,400 00
" " National Vessels, ...	20,000 00
All other Ports, all vessels, cargoes and supplies, estimated, . .	30,000 00
	$1,354,122 02

Total of all Exports, Port of Honolulu.

Value Foreign Goods exported, ...	$355.539 85
Value Domestic Goods exported, ...	1,205,622 02
Value Domestic Goods furnished as Supplies, ...	118,500 00
	$1,679,661 87

Value of Goods paying duty Imported at Honolulu, from

United States, Pacific side, ...	$669,015 96
United States, Atlantic side, ...	137,486 87
Bremen, ...	213,097 39
Great Britain, ...	164,614 45
British Columbia, ...	14,037 11
Sea, ...	4,153 71
Islands of the Pacific, ...	698,70
Russian Possessions, ...	4,409 63
Sydney, ...	168 00
Hongkong, ...	˙23,739 15
Tahiti, ...	302,30
Japan, ...	173 50
	$1,231,896 17

Value of Goods, Including Spirits, Bonded from

United States, Pacific side,	$119,260 24
United States, Atlantic side,	137,009 54
Bremen,	17,411 74
Great Britain,	48,547 86
British Columbia,	7,322 19
Sea,	205,617 11
Islands of the Pacific,	13,793 10
Russian Possessions,	27,413 56
Sydney,	2,709 80
Hongkong,	404 35
Tahiti,	916 80
Guam,	2,502 87
	$582,909 16

Resume---Imports.

Value of goods paying duties,	$1,231,896 77
" and spirits bonded,	582,909 16
" imported free,	133,463 31
" imported at Lahaina, duty paid,	2,613 59
" " Hilo, duty paid,	3,135 55
" " " free,	2,871 86
" " Kawaihae, duty paid,	113 05
" " " free,	214 18
" " Kealakeakua "	192 70
	$1,957,410 17

Merchant Vessels and Steamers at the Ports of the Hawaiian Islands, 1867.

NATION.	HONOLULU.				LAHAINA.		HILO.		TOTALS.	
	INSIDE.		OUTSIDE.							
	No.	Tons.	No.	Tons.	No.	Tons.	No.	Tons.	No.	Tons.
American,	54	24,283	11	9,344	1	572	3	708	69	34,862
British,	24	11,495	6	4,900	..	....	1	225	31	16,620
Hawaiian,	29	6,503	..	....	..	....	..	....	29	6,503
Russian,	1	612	1	772	..	....	..	....	2	1,384
Norwegian,	..	....	1	437	..	....	..	....	1	437
French,	..	....	1	393	..	....	..	....	1	393
Tahitian,	1	69	..	....	..	....	..	....	1	69
	109	42,962	20	15,846	1	527	4	933	134	60,268

Whaling Vessels at the Ports of Hawaiian Islands, 1867.

NATION.	HONOLULU.		Lahaina.	Hilo.	Kawaihae	Totals.
	INSIDE.	OUTSIDE.				
American, ...	76	54	10	38	49	227
Hawaiian, ...	6	..	..	1	..	7
Oldenburg, ...	3	..	..	..	..	3
British, ...	..	..	..	1	..	1
French, ...	1	1	..	..	1	3
Tahitian, ...	1	1	..	..	..	2
	87	56	10	40	50	243

NOTE.

The Catalogue of Hawaiian Publications here presented was suggested by Mr. J. F. Hunnewell, and as many books in the native language were fast passing away, it seemed worth the while to collect such titles as might now be found. The former catalogues of Dibble, Jarves, Pease and Martin have been here rearranged, and a large collection of Island publications, procured for Harvard College through the kindness of the Hawaiian Evangelical Board and individual missionaries, has been added. To economize space, the catalogue has been arranged under authors, and where these are unknown, under subjects, so that in no case is the same title repeated; cross references are, however, given.

The list of works relating to the Islands in the Library of Harvard College (marked H. C. in the Catalogue), was chiefly made by Sanford B. Dole, Esq., and the index to the Missionary Herald by Mr. J. F. Hunnewell, who has also rendered much assistance in other ways. Books found only in his collection are marked H.

Books collected by the compiler are marked B., and all such in the Hawaiian language have been deposited in the Harvard Library, where is now the largest collection of Hawaiian literature extant. A few (marked A.) are in the Boston Athenæum. Publications of the American Mission, embracing two hundred and thirty-eight titles, are, except those printed at Lahainaluna, marked M., those of the Catholic Mission, C. M., and some others, H. M. W. (H. M. Whitney).

It is hoped that omissions and additions as well as corrections, will be reported to the officers of the Hawaiian Club, that as complete a list, especially of Hawaiian Works, as possible may be preserved.

A CATALOGUE OF WORKS

PUBLISHED AT, OR RELATING TO,

THE HAWAIIAN ISLANDS.

AGRICULTURAL SOCIETY, ROYAL HAWAIIAN, TRANSACTIONS OF. *Honolulu*, 1850-56. 2 vols. 8vo. B. (H. C.)

AHA ELELE, KA.—The Convention. A Journal published in American and Hawaiian during the debates in the Convention of 1864. 18 Nos. to August 31. *Honolulu.*

AI O KA LA, KA.—Daily Food. 2d Edition. *New York*, 1862. 18mo. pp. 154. (A. B. C. F. M.) B. See Emerson.

ALAKAI MUA.—First steps in Reading. *Honolulu*,1854. 12mo. B. (H.C.)

ALAULA, KE.—A Child's Paper. Illus. *Honolulu*, 1866.

ALEMANAKA HAWAII. *Honolulu*, 1834. 2000 copies.

ALEMANAKA KERITIANO, 1861. *Honolulu*, M., 1861. 12mo. pp. 36. B. (H. C.)

Almanacs have been published every year since 1835.

ALEXANDER (WILLIAM DEWITT). — A short synopsis of the most essential points in Hawaiian Grammar : for the use of the pupils of Oahu College. *Honolulu*, H. M. W., 1864. 2 pts. pp. 19 and 34. 12mo. B. (H. C.)

——— Review of a Pastoral Address by T. N. Staley; containing a reply to some of his charges against the American Protestant Mission to the Hawaiian Islands. [Originally published in the Pacific Commercial Advertiser.] *Honolulu*, H. M. W., 1864. 8vo. pp. 87. B. (H. C.)

ALEXANDER, (Rev. W. P.).—Na Haawina mua o ka hoailona helu, a me ka anahonua, ka ana huinakolu, ka anaaina, a me ke kumu holoholo moku. [Translated from Legendre.] *Lahainaluna*, 1843.

——— Na Hoike e ikeia'i i ka olelo i kapaia o ka Palapala Hemolele. [Biblical Commentary.] *Honolulu*, M., 1849. 12mo. B.

ALEXANDER (Rev. W. P.).—Same. 2d Edition. *Honolulu*, H. M. W., 1863. 12mo. pp. 116. B. (H. C.)

—— He olelo no ke Akua ano, a me na mea ana i kauoha mai ai i kanaka. A Treatise on God's character, and commandments to men. *Honolulu*, M., 1848. 12mo. pp. 219. B. (H. C.)

—— 2d Edition. *Honolulu*, H. M. W., 1861. B. (H. C.)

—— ARMSTRONG and CLARK. Matematcka. *Lahainaluna*, 1838. 8vo. pp. 168. B. (H. C.)

ALLEN (ELISHA H.).—See Reports.

AMATEUR, THE.—Edited by A. M. Carter. Aug., 1852. Published by the "Hawaiian Juvenile Society."

ANAHONUA, KE.—Trigonometry. *Lahainaluna*, 1834. 8vo. pp. 122. 45 woodcuts. B. (H. C.)

—— See Andrews, Lorrin.

. ANDERSON.—A Catalogue of the different species of cloth collected in the three voyages of Captain Cook, with a particular account of the manner of manufacturing the same in the various islands of the South Seas; extracted from observations of Anderson and R. Forster. *London*, 1787. 4to.

ANDERSON (Mrs. E. H.).—He mau olelo i na wahine o Hawaii. Address to the Women of Hawaii. *Honolulu*, H. M. W., 1863. 18mo. 12. B. (H. C.)

✗ ANDERSON (Miss M. E.).—Scenes in the Hawaiian Islands and California. *Boston*, 1861. 18mo. pp. 238. Illus.

ANDERSON (Rev. RUFUS).—Memorial volume of the first Fifty Years of the American Board of Commissioners for Foreign Missions. *Boston*, 1861. Fifth Ed. 1863. 8vo. pp. 450. Map and Woodcuts. B. (H. C.)

✗ —— The Hawaiian Islands, their Progress and Condition under Missionary Labors. *Boston*, Gould & Lincoln, 1864. 12mo. pp. 450. Map and woodcuts. B. (H. C.)

—— Special Report presented to the A. B. C. F. M., Sept., 1866, on the Reformed Catholics and Sandwich Islands Mission. 8vo. pp. 8. B. (H. C.)

—— Sermon at Funeral of Rev. E. Spaulding. *Boston*, 1840. 8vo. H.

ANDERSSON (N. J.).— Botanique du Voyage de la frégate suédoise *l'Eugenie*, en 1851–53. *Stockholm*, 1857. 4to, plates.

—— See Virgin (C. A.).

ANDREWS (Rev. LORRIN).—Ka Hoike Honua. Geography. *Honolulu*, M., 1832. 12mo. pp. 44. 3d Ed. B.

—— Na Holoholona o ka Honua. Animals of the World. *Honolulu*, M., 1833. 12mo. pp. 12, with a chart. B. (H. C.)

ANDREWS (Rev. LORRIN).—Ke Anahonua, *Honolulu*, M., 1833. 18mo. pp. 61. Illus. B. (H. C.)
—— 2d Edition. *Honolulu*, 1854. B. (II. C.)
—— Olelo Hoakaka no ka Honua. Questions on Geography. *Honolulu*, M., 1834. B.
—— He mau haawina no ka Palapala Hemolele. Bible Class Book, from Abbott and Fiske. Vol. I. *Lahainaluna*, 1834. 16mo. pp. 100. B.
—— Ka Hoikehonua a me Palapala aina. *Lahainaluna*, 1835. pp. 216. B. (II. C.)
—— A Vocabulary of the Hawaiian Language. *Lahainaluna*, 1835–36. 8vo. pp. 132. B.
—— Palapala aina. Atlas of colored maps. *Lahainaluna*, 1836. 4to. pp. 9. 3d Ed. B.
—— Maps of Sacred Geography. *Lahainaluna*, 1837. pp. 6. 2d Ed. B. (H. C.)
—— Palapala Hakau Kii. Drawing. *Lahainaluna*, 1837. 12mo. pp. 36. B. (II. C.)
—— He Mau Haawina no ka olelo Beritania. Lessons on the English language. *Lahainaluna*, 1837. 12mo. pp. 36.
—— 2d Edition. *Lahainaluna*, 1841. 12mo. pp. 40. B. (H. C.)
—— 3d Edition. *Honolulu*, 1844. B. (H. C.)
—— Grammar. American and Hawaiian. *Lahainaluna*, 1837. 8vo. pp. 40.
—— Kumu kahiki. Foreign Primer. *Lahainaluna*, 1837. 12mo. pp. 36. B. (II. C.)
—— Sermon preached at Lahainaluna, October 18th, 1839, on the death of Mr. Charles McDonald. *Lahainaluna*, 1840. 8vo. pp. 31. B. (II. C.)
—— He mau Palapala aina. *Lahainaluna*, 1840. 4to., atlas, col. B. (II. C.)
—— English and Hawaiian Lessons. *Lahainaluna*, 1841. 16mo. pp. 40. B. (H. C.)
—— Hoike Honua. Keith's Study of the Globes. *Lahainaluna*, 1841. 16mo. pp. 80. B. (H. C.)
—— Hoike Honua a me Palapala aina no ka olelo a ke Akua. *Lahainaluna*, 1842. 4to. 6 maps col. B. (II. C.)
—— He mau Palapala aina a me na niele e pili ana. 2d Edition. *Lahainaluna*, 1840. Colored Maps. B. (II. C.)
—— O ke kokua no ko Hawaii poe kamalii e ao i ka olelo Beritania. Exercise Book for Hawaiian Children learning English. *Lahainaluna*, 1843. 18mo. pp. 104. B. (II. C.)

Andrews (Rev. Lorrin).—Grammar of the Hawaiian Language. *Honolulu*, M., 1854. 8vo. pp. 158. B.

―――― A Dictionary of the Hawaiian Language, to which is appended an English Hawaiian Vocabulary, and a Chronological Table of Remarkable Events. *Honolulu*, H. M. W., 1865. 8vo. pp. 560. B.

―――― Green (Rev. J. S.) Palapala Helubelu. Reading Book. *Lahainaluna*, 1842. 12mo. pp. 340.

―――― Sabbath Whaling. Hawaiian Tract Society. No. 1. n. d. 18mo. pp. 20. B. (II. C.)

Andrews (Samuel C.).—Ke Keiki Paionia, or Pioneer Boy. I unuhiia a i kakauiia ma ka olelo Hawaii. *Lahainaluna*, 1868.

Aniani, Te. *Honolulu*, C. M., 1858. 8vo. pp. 19. B. (II. C.)

Aohoku, O ke. *Lahainaluna*, n. d. 12mo. pp. 12. (A. B. C. F. M.)

Ao kiko; oia ke ao ana i ke kau ana i na kiko, a me ka hookomo ana i na hua nui ma ka olelo. A Treatise on Punctuation. *Honolulu*, M., n. d. 12mo. pp. 24. B. (II. C.)

Arago (Jacques).—Promenade autour du monde pendant les années 1817-18-19-20, sur les corvettes du roi *l'Uranie* et *la Physicienne*, commandées par M. Freycinet. *Paris*, Leblanc, 1823. 2 vols in 8vo, et atlas in fol. de 26 pl.

x ―――― English translation. *London*, Treultel & Wurtz, 1823. 4to. Illus. See p. 56 to p. 153. (II. C.)

―――― Souvenirs d'un aveugle, voyage autour du monde. *Paris*, Gayet, 1838. 4 vols. gr. in 8vo.

―――― ―――― Third Edition, enrichie de 60 dessins exécutés par M. Maurin, et de notes scientifique par M. F. Arago. *Paris*, 1840. 4 vols. gr. in 8vo.

Arnott (G. A. W.).—See Hooker and Arnott.

Armstrong (Rev. R.).—Olelo no ka ano Pope. On Popery. *Honolulu*, M., 1841. 12mo. pp. 23.

―――― Obituary Notice of Mrs. Angeline L. Castle. *Honolulu*, M., 1841. 12mo. pp. 12. (A. B. C. F. M.)

―――― Moral Philosophy translated from Wayland. *Lahainaluna*, 1841. 12mo. pp. 215. B. (H. C.)

―――― and Dibble (Rev. S.). Ka Wchewehchala. On Depravity. *Honolulu*, M., 1847. 12mo. pp. 288. B. (II. C.)

Athenaeum Français.—(1852, p. 215;—1853, p. 39;—1855, pp. 842, 939;—1856, p. 362.)

Audience granted by the King to William Miller, Esquire, H. B. M.'s Consul General, Anthony Ten Eyck, Esquire, United States Commissioner, and William Patrick Dillon, Esquires, Consul of France, etc. *Honolulu*, 1848. 8vo. pp. 16.

Au Okoa.—Weekly, published by the Government since January, 1865.

Aylmer (Capt. Fenton).—A Cruise in the Pacific, from the log of a Naval Officer. *London*, 1860. 2 vols.

Ayr Advertiser.—November 1, 1861. Historical sketch of the progress of the Hawaiian Government since 1845.

Bachelot (M. Alexis).—Lettres du Préfet Apostolique des Iles Sandwich. [Annales de la Propagation de la Foi. 1830, p. 274, et 1835, p. 16.]

———— Lettre contenant le détail de l'expulsion des Missionaries des Iles Sandwich. (Lithographed.)

Baibala.—See Bible.

Baldwin (Dr. D.).—No ka ona ano. On Intemperance. *Honolulu*, M., 1838. 12mo. pp. 28.

Ball (Z.).—Remarks on the Geological Features of Oahu, Sandwich Islands. [Silliman's Journal, XXVIII, p. 15.]

Barrot (Adolphe).—Les Iles Sandwich. [Revue des Deux Mondes, 1er et 15me août 1839.]

The articles of M. Barrot have been translated into American by the Rev. Daniel Dole, and published in "The Friend," *Honolulu*, 1850.

Barrow (John).—Captain Cook's Voyages of Discovery. *Edinburgh*, 1860. This Abridgement contains unedited materials from the Admiralty Archives.

Bates (George Washington).—Sandwich Island Notes, by a Haole. *New York*, Harper & Bros., 1854. 12mo. Illus. B.

Beckwith (Rev. E. G.).—Inauguration of, as President of Oahu College, at the Court House in Honolulu, Sept. 25, 1854. *Honolulu*, M., 1854. 12mo. pp. 217. B. (H. C.)

Beechey (Capt. F. W.).—Narrative of a Voyage to the Pacific and Behring's Straits, to coöperate with the polar expeditions; performed in H. M. ship *Blossom*, under the command of Capt. F. W. Beechey, in 1825-26-27-28. *London*, Murray, 1831. 4to., figures and charts. (H. C.) See pp. 229-235.

———— Another Edition. *London*, 1831. 2 vols. 8vo.

Beechey arrived at Honolulu the 19th of May, 1826, left on the 31st for the Arctic Ocean, returned on the 26th of January, 1827, and sailed on the 4th of March for the East Indies.

Belcher (Sir Edward).—Narrative of a Voyage around the World, performed in H. M. ship *Sulphur*, 1836-42, etc. *London*, 1843. 2 vols. 8vo. Maps and plates.

BELCHER (Sir EDWARD).—Proceedings of H. B. M. ship *Sulphur* in the Pacific Ocean. [Nautical Magazine and Naval Chronicle.] London, 1838.

> Belcher was at Honolulu from the 8th to the 27th of July, 1837, and from the 30th of May to the 16th of June, 1839.

BELCHER (J. H.).—Around the World; a narrative of a voyage in the East India Squadron, under Commodore George C. Read. *New York*, 1840. 2 vols. 8vo.

BENNETT (E. T.).—On some Fishes from the Sandwich Islands. *London*, 1820. 8vo. 10 plates.

BENNETT (GEORGE).—See Tyerman and Bennett.

λ BENNETT (F. DEBELL).—Narrative of a Whaling Voyage round the globe, from 1833–36, comprising sketches of Polynesia, California, the Indian Archipelago, etc. With an account of Southern Whales, the Sperm Whale Fishery, and the Natural History of the countries visited. *London*, 1840. 2 vols. 8vo. Frontis. and Map.

——— Second Edition. *London*, 1842. 2 vols. 8vo.

> Bennett arrived the 16th of April, 1834, and remained five weeks; returned on the 2d of October, left on the 20th, and again spent a month from October 4th, 1835.

BENTHAM (G.).—Botany of the Voyage of H. M. Ship *Sulphur* in 1836–42; edited and superintended by T. Brinsley Hinds. *London*, 1844. 4to. Atlas of 60 plates.

BERESFORD.—See Dixon.

BERITA HOOLILO O KA EKALESIA HAWAII, KA.—12mo. pp. 4. n. d. (*Honolulu*, 1821?)

BERNHARDI (Madame CHARLOTTE).—See Krusenstern.

BIBLE. KA PALAPALA HEMOLELE.—Various portions of the Bible were published before the whole was translated. The complete editions are as follows:—

> Ke Kauoha hou a ko kakou Haku e ola'i, a Iesu Kristo: oia ka olelo hemolele no ke ola, a na lunaolelo i kakau ai. Ua unuhiia mai ka olelo Helene. Ua paiia na ko Amerika poe i huiia e hoolaha i ka Baibala. *Honolulu*, M., 1837. 12mo. pp. 520.
> Ka Palapala Hemolele a Iehova ko kakou Akua. O ke Kauoha kahiko i unuhiia mai ka olelo Hebera. Buke I, Buke II. Paiia no ko Amerika poe hoolaha Baibala. (*Oahu, Honolulu*), M., 1838. pp. 924, 887. [Dated at end, May 10th, 1839.]
> Three volumes generally bound in one of pp. 2331. B. (II. C.) II.
> Ka Palapala Hemolele a Iehova ko kakou Akua. O ke Kauoha kahiko a me ke Kauoha hou i unuhiia mailoko mai o na olelo

— 69 —

kahiko. Paiia no ko Amerika poe hoolaha Baibala. *Honolulu*, 1843. 8vo. pp. 1451.
The same in 4to.
Ke Kauoha hou a'ko kakou Haku e ola'i a Iesu Kristo na unuhiia mai ka olelo Helene, a ua hooponopono hou ia. *Nu Yoka*. Paiia no ko Amerika poe hoolaha Baibala, 1857. In Hawaiian and English. 12mo. pp. 727.
Ka Baibala Hemolele o ke Kauoha kahiko a me ke Kauoha hou; i unuhiia mailoko mai o na olelo kahiko a ua hooponopono hou ia. *Nu Yoka*. Paiia no ko Amerika poe hoolaha Baibala, 1868. Roy. 8vo. and 4to. pp. 1456.
A revised translation, with marginal references.
An Edition of this translation of the New Testament (Kauoha hou) in 18mo, is in press (1868).

BICKNELL (Rev. J.).—He Hamani pia pa. Primer in Marquesan. *Honolulu*, M., 1858. 12mo. pp. 48. B. (H. C.)
—— Te Evanelia i patutea e Ioane. Gospel of St. John in Marquesan. *Honolulu*, M., 1858. 12mo. pp. 98. B. (H. C.)

BILLECOCQ.—See Meares.

BINGHAM (Rev. HIRAM).—Kumu mua. First Lessons in Reading and Spelling. *Honolulu*, M., 1822-25. 12mo. pp. 8. 10th Ed. 1832. 180,900 copies. B. (H. C.)
—— He Palapala mua na na Kamalii. First Book for Children. *Honolulu*, M., 1830. 18mo. pp. 36. 3d Edition.
—— He Ninau Hoike, no ka mooolelo o ka Palapala Hemolele. Scripture Catechism. *Honolulu*, M., 1831.
—— 2d Edition. 1832. With woodcuts.
—— 3d Edition. 1864. 24mo. pp. 189. B. (H. C.)
x —— Bartimeus, or the Sandwich Islands. American Tract Society. n. d.
x —— Fall of Meteorites at the Sandwich Islands. [Silliman's American Journal of Science. Vol. XLIX, p. 407.]
—— A Residence of twenty-one years in the Sandwich Islands, or the Civil, Religious and Political History of those Islands; containing a particular view of the Missionary operations connected with the Introduction of Christianity and Civilization among the Hawaiian People. *Hartford* and *New York*, 1847. 8vo. pp. 616. B. Map and woodcuts.

BINGHAM (Rev. HIRAM, Jr.).—Te Boke ni wareware. Primer in Gilbert Islands Dialect. *Honolulu*, 1860. 18mo. pp. 20. Illus. B. (H. C.)
—— Ana Taeka napaukai ara uwea ao ara Tiakamaiu Ieso Kristo. First XII. chaps. Matthew, in Apaiana Dialect. *Honolulu*.

BISHOP (Rev. ARTEMAS).—Ke Helu Kamalii, translated from Fowle's Child's Arithmetic. *Honolulu*, M., 1833. 24mo. pp. 6. 4th Edition.

―――― Helunaau. Mental Arithmetic, from Colburn. *Lahainaluna*, 1834. 18mo. pp. 132. 4th Edition.

―――― Ka hope no ka Helunaau. Colburn's Sequel. *Honolulu*, M., 1835. 12mo. pp. 116. 2d Edition. B. (H. C.)

―――― Haawina o ka hoailona Helu. From Colburn's Algebra. *Lahainaluna*, 1838. 12mo. pp. 44.

―――― Ka Hele Malihini Ana, mai keia oa aku, chiki i kela ao. He olelouhane i hookalikeia me ke mocuhanela. Na Ioane Buniana. Pilgrim's Progress. *Honolulu*, M., 1842. 16mo. pp. 410. 8 woodcuts. B. (H. C.)

―――― Haawina mua o ka hoailona helu. Translated from Bailey's Algebra. *Lahainaluna*, 1843. 8vo. pp. 160. B. (H. C.)

―――― 2d Edition. *Boston*, 1858.

―――― 3d Edition. *Honolulu*, 1865.

―――― He Huina Helu. Oia ka helunaau, me ka kelu kakau i huiia. A general Arithmetic. Translated from Geo. Leonard. *Honolulu*, M., 1852. 12mo. pp. 204. B. (H. C.)

―――― Na Huaolelo a me na olelo kikeke ma ka Beritania a me ka olelo Hawaii, no na Haumana e ao ana i kela a me keia. A Manual of Conversations, Hawaiian and English. Hawaiian Phrase Book. *Honolulu*, H. M. W., 1854. 16mo. pp. 112. B.

―――― See Emerson and Bishop.

BOPP (F.).—Ueber die Verwandtsschaft der Malayischpolynesischen Sprachen mit der Indisch-europæischen. *Berlin*, 1841. 4to.

BOTANY.— See Anderson, Bentham, Breckenridge, Brigham, Brongniart, Gaudichaud, Gray, Hooker, Kittlitż, Langsdorff, Mann.

BRANDT (J. T.).—Prodromus descriptionis Animalium ab H. Mertensio, in orbis terrarum Circumnavigatione, observatorum. *St. Petersburg*, 1835. 4to.

BRECKENRIDGE (W. D.).—Botany of the United States Exploring Expedition. Cryptogamia, Filices including Lycopodiaceæ, and Hydropterides. *Philadelphia*. 4to., with fol. Atlas of 46 plates.

Scarce, as the edition was destroyed by fire.

BRIGHAM (WILLIAM T.).—Recent Investigations on the Hawaiian Volcanoes. [Proceedings of the Boston Society of Natural History. Vol. XI. p. 17.]

―――― A visit to the Volcano of Kilauea. [American Naturalist. Vol. I. p. 16.]

— 71 —

BRIGHAM (WILLIAM T.).—Notes on the Volcanoes of the Hawaiian Islands. With a History of their various Eruptions. *Boston*, 1868. 4to. pp. 132. 5 maps and 47 woodcuts. [Memoirs Boston Society of Natural History. Vol. I., Pt. III.]

——— Notes on Hesperomannia; a new genus of Hawaiian Compositæ. *Boston*. 1868. 4to. pp. 2, plate. [Memoirs Boston Society of Natural History. Vol. I., Pt. IV.]

——— See Remy.

BRINSMADE (P. A.).—Case of Libel *vs.* J. J. Jarves. *Honolulu*, 1846. 8vo.

BRONGNIART et DECAISNE.—Botanique du voyage autour du monde sur *la Vénus*, en 1838-39. *Paris*, Gide, 1841-49. 8vo, et atlas de 28 pl.

BROUGHTON (W. R.).—Voyage of discovery in the *Dædalus*, to the North Pacific Ocean, 1795-98, in which the coast of Asia, from Lat. 35° N. to 52° N., etc., have been examined and surveyed. *London*, 1804. 4to. Map and 9 plates.

——— Voyage de découverte dans la partie septentrionale de l'Océan Pacifique, fait par le capitaine W. R. Broughton, pendant les années 1795-98; trad. de l'anglais par T. B. Eyriès. *Paris*, Dentu, 1807. 2 vols. 8vo. Fig. et cartes.

Broughton arrived at Waimea, Kauai, the 3d of February, 1796, and touched again at the Islands on his return from the coast of America.

BULLETIN DE LA SOCIÉTÉ DE GÉOGRAPHIE DE PARIS.—Reports and Notices relating to the Islands.

1ʳᵉ Série: t. III, pp. 143, 156;—IV, 206;—V, 611 à 633;—VI, 154 à 163;—IX, 192, 232, 234;—XI, 128;—XII, 96;—XIV, 164;—XV, 224, 235, 236, 256;—XVI, 272;—XVII, 1 à 21.

2ᵉ Série: t. V, p. 161;—XXI, 170, 171;—XIX, 50, 53, 344;—XX, 338, 341, 344.

3ᵉ Série: t. VII, p. 54;—VIII, 221;—X, 22.

4ᵉ Série: t. IV, p. 10;—VI, 153;—VIII, 245, 366.

5ᵉ Série: t. VII, p. 111;—XII, 208 à 228.

BYRON (Capt. Lord G. A.).— Narrative of the voyage of H. M. ship *Blonde* to the Sandwich Islands, in 1824-25, for the purpose of conveying the bodies of their late King and Queen to their native country. (With an Introduction by Mrs. Maria Graham.) *London*, Murray, 1827. 4to. pp. 260. Fig.

Byron anchored at Lahaina, May 24th, 1825, visited Honolulu and Hilo, and sailed July 18th.

CACIQUE.—Shipment of Sandal-wood to China. *Macao*, 1845.
CALKIN (M.).—See Church Music.

⨯ CAMPBELL (ARCHIBALD).—Voyage around the world, 1806-12, in which Japan, Kamschatka .... and the Sandwich Islands were visited; including a narrative of the author's shipwreck ....; with an account of the present state of the Sandwich Islands, and a Vocabulary of their Language. *Edinburgh*, 1816. 8vo. pp. 288. Map. (II. C.)
    Campbell arrived at Hawaii the 27th of January, 1809, and remained at the Islands until March 4th, 1810.

CAMPBELL (JOHN).—Maritime Discoveries and Christian Missions, considered in their natural relations. *London*, 1840. 8vo.

CASSIN (JOHN).—Mammalia and Ornithology of the United States Exploring Expedition. *Philadelphia*, 1858. 4to. Atlas fol. 53 pl.

——— On the Genus Mohoa. [Proceedings of the Philadelphia Academy, 1855. Vol. VII. p. 440.]

CASTERA.—See Kippis.

CASTLE (S. N.). — An account of the Transactions connected with the visit of the *Artémise*. Remarks on the Manifesto and the Treatment of the Missionaries. *Honolulu*, 1839. 8vo. pp. 14. Other copies. pp. 63. (A. B. C. F. M.)

CATHOLIC PRIESTS.—Statement in regard to the Introduction of Catholic Priests in 1826. By an old Resident. [Boston Mercantile Journal, Feb. 14th, 1840.]

——— Supplement to "S. I. Mirror" containing an account of the Persecutions of Catholics at the Sandwich Islands. *Honolulu*, R. I. Howard, Jan. 15th, 1840. 8vo. pp. 100. Curious cuts, by J. Dudoit. A.

CHAMISSO (ADELBERT VON).—Reise um die Welt mit der Romanzoffischen Entdeckungs-Expedition, in den Jahren 1815-18, auf der Brigg *Rurick*, Capt. Otto von Kotzebue. *Leipzig*, 1836. 2 vols. 12mo. Maps and portrait.

——— De Animalibus quibusdam e Classe Vermium (Linné), in Circumnavigatione terræ, duce Otho de Kotzebue, annis 1815-18 peracta, observatis. *Berlin*, 1819. 4to.

——— Ueber die Hawaiische Sprache. [Vorgelegt der Königlichen Akademie der Wissenschaften zu Berlin am 12 Januar, 1837.] *Leipzig*, Weidemann, 1837. 4to.

CHART OF SACRED HISTORY. — *Lahainaluna*, n. d. 4to. Copper plates. B. (II. C.)

CHARTS.—Those published by the United States Exploring Expedition are the only even tolerably correct ones.

— 73 —

CHEEVER (Rev. H. T.).—Life in the Sandwich Islands, or the Heart of the Pacific, as it Was and Is. *New York*, 1851. 12mo. Illus.

—— Island World in the Pacific; being the Personal Narrative and Results of Travel through the Sandwich Islands. *New York*, 1851. 8vo.

—— The Sandwich or Hawaiian Islands, their History and Relations to the rest of the World. *New York*, Biblical Repository, July, 1849.

—— 2d Edition. *London*, Bentley, 1851, 8vo.; and *New York*, 12mo. (H. C.)

CHEVALIER (E.).—Minéralogie et Géologie du Voyage autour du monde, en 1836–37, sur *la Bonite*. *Paris*, Arthus Bertrand, 1844. 8vo. pl.

—— See Darondeau et E. Chevalier.

CHORIS (LOUIS).—Voyage pittoresque autour du monde, offrant des portraits des sauvages d'Amérique, d'Asie, d'Afrique et du grand Océan, leurs armes, leurs habillements, parures, ustensils . . . . des paysages et des vues maritimes, plusieurs objects d'histoire naturelle . . . . accompagnés de descriptions par M. le baron Cuvier, etc., le tout dessiné par M. Louis Choris, dans le voyage qu'il a fait de 1815–1818; lithographié par lui-même et d'autres artistes. *Paris*, Choris (imprim. de Firmin Didot), 1821–23. Fol. 110 pl.

—— Vues et paysages des régions équinoxiales, recueillis dans un voyage autour du monde, avec un introduction et une description des planches. *Paris*, Arthus Bertrand, 1826. Pet. in fol. avec 24 planches.

Choris was the artist of Kotzebue's Expedition.

CHURCH MUSIC.—Hawaiian Collection of, compiled for the use of Foreign Communities at the Sandwich Islands, by M. Calkin, J. F. B. Marshall and F. Johnson. *Honolulu*, 1840. Oblong 8vo. pp. 147.

CLARK (Rev. E. W.).—He olelo no ka Mare ana. A Tract on Marriage. *Honolulu*, M., 1833. 12mo. pp. 12. B. (H. C.)

—— He hoike na Hoku. Astronomy. *Lahainaluna*, 1837. 12mo. pp. 12.

—— O ke Akeakamai; no na Kamalii. The Little Philosopher. From Abbott. *Lahainaluna*, 1837. 12mo. pp. 40.

—— and RICHARDS. Hawaiian Almanac. *Honolulu*, M., 1835. 8vo. pp. 16.

—— See Alexander, Armstrong and Clark, and Green and Clark.

CLARK (Dr. SAMUEL).—O na olelo hoopomaikai o ka Palapala Hemolele. *New York*, American Tract Society, 1858. 12mo. pp. 309. B. (H. C.)

CLEVELAND (RICHARD J.).—A Narrative of Voyages and Commercial Enterprises. *Cambridge, Mass.*, John Owen, 1842. 2 vols. 12mo. (II. C.)

——— 2d Edition. *London*, 1842.

——— 3d Edition. *Boston*, 1850.

    Cleveland spent the 19th of July, 1799, at the Islands, and returned June 16th, 1803, remaining until July 9th. He imported the first horses. See North American Review, July, 1842.

COAN (Rev. TITUS).—On Kilauea. [Silliman's Journal (2) XII. pp. 80–82, 1851.]

——— Eruption of Mauna Loa, 1851. [*Ibid.* XIII. pp. 395–397.]

——— "   "   " 1852. [*Ibid.* XIV. pp. 205, 219–224.]

——— Kilauea and the recent eruption of Mauna Loa, 1852. [*Ibid.* XV. pp. 63–65.]

——— Present condition of Kilauea, 1854. [*Ibid.* XVIII. pp. 96–98.]

——— Kilauea, 1855. [*Ibid.* XX. pp. 100–102.]

——— Recent eruption, 1855. [*Ibid.* XXI. pp. 237–241.]

——— Eruption at Hawaii, 1856. [*Ibid.* XXII. pp. 240–243.]

    See also " Missionary Herald."

CODE OF ETIQUETTE.—Order in Council of H. H. Majesty prescribing. June 29th, 1844. In Hawaiian and English. *Honolulu*. 12mo. pp. 18.

✕ COKE (H. J.).—A Ride over the Rocky Mountains to Oregon and California, with a glance at some of the Tropical Islands, including the West Indies and the Sandwich Islands. *London*, 1852. 8vo.

✕ COLNETT (Capt. JAMES).—Voyage to the South Atlantic, and round Cape Horn into the Pacific Ocean, for the purpose of extending the Spermaceti Whale Fisheries and other objects of commerce, by ascertaining the Ports, Bays, Harbors and Anchoring Berths in certain Islands and Coasts in those seas. *London*, 1798. 4to. Fig. and 9 maps.

——— Account of a voyage in the Pacific, made in 1793–94. *London*, 1804. 4to.

    Colnett visited the Islands several times and introduced the sheep, landing a ram and ewe at Waimea, Kauai.

COLTON (Rev. WALTER).—Deck and Port, or Incidents of a Cruise in the U. S. Frigate *Congress* to California; with sketches of Rio Janeiro, Valparaiso, Honolulu and San Francisco. *New York*, 1850. 12mo. (H. C.)

✗ Comettant (Oscar).—Les Civilizations inconnues. *Paris*, Pagnerre, 1863. 18mo.

    See page 73 and below, articles of no historical value previously published in the Siècle.

Constitution and Laws of his Majesty Kamehameha III., King of the Hawaiian Islands. Passed by the Nobles and Representatives at their Session, 1852. 8vo. pp. 88. *Honolulu*, by order of the Legislature, 1852. B. (H. C.)

Constitution granted by H. M. Kamehameha V., by the Grace of God King of the Hawaiian Islands, on the twentieth day of August, A. D., 1864. *Honolulu*, 1864. 8vo.

——— See Kumu Kanawai.

——— and By-laws of the First Hawaiian Guard, instituted November, 1852. *Honolulu*, 1852. 12mo.

——— of the Original Hawaiian Church. October 15th, 1819. 12mo. pp. 4. *Honolulu?* (A. B. C. F. M.)

✗ Consular Grievances, Table of, 1843-46. *Honolulu*, 1862. 8vo. Not published.

Convention.—See Aha Elele.

✗ Cook (Capt. James).—A Voyage to the Pacific Ocean, undertaken by command of His Majesty, for making discoveries in the Northern Hemisphere; performed under the direction of Captains Cook, Clerke and Gore, on H. M. Ships *Resolution* and *Discovery*, in the years 1776-80. Vols. I. and II. written by Capt. James Cook; Vol. III. by Capt. James King. Published by order of the Lords Commissioners of the Admiralty. *London*, 1784. 3 vols. in 4to. 1 vol. folio of 87 plates. (H. C.)

——— 2d Edition. *London*, 1785. 3 vols. 4to.

    Published by Dr. Douglas, afterwards Bishop of Salisbury. Plates executed under the supervision of Jos. Banks.

✗ ——— Troisième Voyage de Cook, où Voyage à l'Ocean Pacifique, exécuté en 1776-80, traduit de l'anglais par M. Demeunier. *Paris*, 1785. 4 vols. 4to. 88 pl.

——— 2d Edition. *Paris*, Moutard, 1785: 3 vols. 18mo.

——— Journal of Capt. Cook's last voyage to the Pacific Ocean, 1776-79. Faithfully narrated from the original MS. *London*, 1781. 8vo. Figs. and maps.

——— Captain Cook's Third and Last Voyage to the Pacific Ocean, in the years 1776-1780. Faithfully abridged from the 4th Edit. Illustrated with copperplates. *London*. 12mo.

——— The Three Voyages of Capt. James Cook round the World. *London*, 1813. 7 vols. 12mo. Figs.

COOK (Capt. JAMES).—The Three Voyages. *London*, 1821. 7 vols. 8vo. Illus.
—— Same. *London*, 1842. 2 vols. 8vo. Illus. s. b.
—— Jac. Cook, Sammlung seiner Reisen um die Welt. *Vienne*, 1804. 3 vols. 8vo.

CORNEY (PETER).—See Choix de Voyages, etc., par J. MacCarthy.
> Corney visited the Islands on the ship *Columbia*, Robson, in March, 1815, again from the 12th of December, 1815, to January 5th, 1816, and finally from the 26th of January to the 6th of April, 1817.

CORRESPONDENCE between H. H. M.'s Sec. of State for Foreign Affairs (R. C. Wyllie) and H. B. M.'s Consul-General (William Miller), on the subject of Richard Charlton's Claim to land. *Honolulu*, 1848, in 8vo.

COUTHOUY (J. P.).—Volcano of Kilauea, Hawaii. [Silliman's Journal. Vol. XLI. p. 200.]
—— Remarks upon Coral Formations in the Pacific. *Boston*, 1842. 8vo. [Boston Journal of Natural History. Vol. IV. pp. 66, 137.]

COUX (H. DE).—Sept. ans en Océanie. Les Rhapsodes et les Conteurs Polynésiens. [Revue contemporaine. T. XXV. p. 465.]

CRAWFURD (JOHN).—On the Malayan and Polynesian Languages and Races. [Journal of the Indian Archipelago and Eastern Asia, April, 1848.]

CUTTS (E. L.).—The Hawaiian or Sandwich Islands. *London*, 1866.

DAILY HAWAIIAN HERALD.—Started Sept. 4th, 1866, only a few numbers printed. *Honolulu.*

DAMON (Rev. S. C.).—A Tribute to the Memory of Hon. William L. Lee, late Chief Justice of the Hawaiian Kingdom. *Honolulu*, H. M. W., 1857. 8vo. pp. 21.
—— Morning Star Papers. 8vo. *Honolulu*, H. M. W., 1861. B. [Supplement to "The Friend."] See "Friend."

DANA (JAMES DWIGHT).—Zoophytes of the United States Exploring Expedition. *Philadelphia*, 1846–49. 4to. Atlas fol. 61 plates.
—— The Crustacea of the United States Exploring Expedition. *Philadelphia*, 1852–55. 2 vols. 4to. Atlas fol. 96 plates. Several colored.
—— Geology of the United States Exploring Expedition. *Philadelphia*, 1849. 4to. Map and woodcuts. Atlas fol. 21 plates.
—— On the Classification and Geographical Distribution of Crustacea. From the Report on Crustacea of the United States Exploring Expedition. *Philadelphia*, 1853. 4to.
—— On Coral Reefs and Islands. *New York*, 1853. 8vo.

DANA (JAMES DWIGHT).—Areas of subsidence in the Pacific indicated by the distribution of Coral Reefs and Islands. [Silliman's Journal, Vol. XIV. pp. 131, 310.

——— Denudation in the Pacific. [*Ibid.* Vol. IX (2). pp. 48-62.]

——— Historical account of the Eruptions on Hawaii. [*Ibid.* Vol. IX (2). pp. 347-364. Vol. X (2). pp. 235-244.]

——— Note on the Eruption of Mauna Loa, 1851. [*Ibid.* Vol. XIV (2). pp. 244-259.]

——— Volcanic action of Mauna Loa. [*Ibid.* Vol. XXI (2). pp. 241-244.]

——— Eruption of Mauna Loa, Hawaii, 1859. [*Ibid.* Vol. XXVII (2). pp. 410-415.]

——— Recent Eruption of Mauna Loa and Kilauea, 1868. [*Ibid.* Vol. XLV (2). pp. 105-123.]

DARONDEAU et E. CHEVALIER.—Physique et Météorologie du Voyage autour du monde exécuté en 1836-37, sur *la Bonite*. *Paris*, 1840-46. 4 vols. 8vo. Illus.

DARWIN (CHARLES).—The Structure and Distribution of Coral Reefs. *London*, 1842. 8vo. Pl. and map.

DAVIS (ROBERT G.).—See Law Reports.

DECAISNE.—See Brongniart et Decaisne.

✗ DELANO (AMASA).—A Narrative of Voyages and Travels in the Northern and Southern Hemispheres; comprising three voyages round the world, together with a voyage of Survey and Discovery in the Pacific Ocean and Oriental Islands. *Boston*, 1817. 8vo. pp. 598. Portrait and views. B.

DEMEUNIER.—See Cook and Vancouver.

DE TESSAN.—Physique et Hydrographie du Voyage autour du monde sur la frégate *la Vénus*, en 1838-39. *Paris*, 1841-49. 5 vols. 8vo. Atlas de 19 cartes.

DIBBLE (Rev. SHELDON).—Dying testimony of believers and unbelievers. *Lahainaluna*, 1832. In Hawaiian. 12mo. pp. 40.

——— He Mooolelo no na holoholona. Na na Kamalii. *Lahainaluna*, 1835. 12mo. pp. 84. 3d Edit.

——— Union Questions. Vol. I. *Lahainaluna*, 1835. 16mo. pp. 156. 2d Ed.

——— Palapala heluhelu, na na Kamalii. *Lahainaluna*, 1835. 12mo. pp. 48. 4th Ed.

——— O ka Hoike honua no ka Palapala Hemolele. Geography of the Bible. *Lahainaluna*, 1835.

——— Second Edition, 1838. 16mo. pp. 84. B. (II. C.) 2000 copies printed.

DIBBLE (Rev. SHELDON).—O ka Hoike manawa a me ke kuhikuhi mooolelo hemolele. Biblical Chronology and History. *Lahainaluna*, 1837. 16mo. pp. 216.

—— Hoike Akua. Natural Theology. Translated from Gallaudet. *Lahainaluna*, 1840. 12mo. pp. 178. Copperplates. B. (H. C.)

—— Second Edition, 1842. Woodcuts. B. (H. C.)

⋋ —— History and General Views of the Sandwich Islands Mission. *New York*, 1839. 12mo. pp. 268. (II. C.)

⋋ —— History of the Sandwich Islands. *Lahainaluna*, 1843. 12mo. pp. 451. (H. C.)

—— Voice from Abroad, or Thoughts on Missions. *New York*, 1844.

—— Hawaiian History. *New York*, 1838. 12mo. pp. 116.

—— Scripture Charts. Six. *Lahainaluna*, 1843.

—— See Armstrong and Dibble.

DIELL (Rev. J.).—Note on the Candlenut Tree (*Aleurites moluccana*). [Silliman's Journal. Vol. XXXIV. p. 209.]

DILLON (Le Chevalier).—Official Correspondence with Chevalier Dillon, Consul of France, relating to charges brought by him against William Paty, Esq., Collector General of Customs, and also relating to the demands made officially by the Consul of France for the repeal of two laws of the Hawaiian Kingdom. *Honolulu*, 1848-49. 8vo. pp. 407. (II. C.)

⤬ DIXON (Capt. GEORGE).—Voyage round the World, etc., but more particularly to the Northwest coast of America, performed in 1785-88. *London*, G. Goulding, 1789. 4to. plates. B. (II. C.) See pp. 50-56 and 90-140.

—— Voyage autour du monde, etc., traduit de l'anglais par Lebas. *Paris*, 1789. 4to.

—— Same. *Paris*, 1789. 2 vols. 8vo. Figs.

The Introduction was by Dixon, the rest by M. Beresford.

—— See Portlock.

DOANE (Rev. EDWARD T.).—Buk in Bwinbwin. Arithmetic in Ebon dialect. *Honolulu*, 1863. 18mo. pp. 24. B. (II. C.)

—— Buk in al. Hymn book in Ebon dialect. *Honolulu*, 1863. 12mo. pp. 24. B. (H. C.)

—— Te Boki n anene ae aiabai Kiritian ni Karaoiroa ti Atua. Apiana. *Honolulu*, H. M. W., 1863. B. (H. C.)

—— Gospel Mak e ar je. Ebon Dialect. *Honolulu*, n. d. 12mo. pp. 24. B. (H. C.)

DOLE (Rev. D.).—See Barrot; also, "Monitor."

DOLE (SANFORD B.).—On a collection of Hawaiian Crania. [Proceedings Boston Society of Natural History. Vol. XI. 1867.]

Dole (Sanford B.).—Catalogue of the described species of Hawaiian Birds. [*Ibid*. Vol. XII.]

Domeny de Rienzi (G. L.). — Océanie. [L'Univers Pittoresque. *Paris*, Didot, 1836.] Many plates. B.

See Vol. II., pp. 10 to 80.

Du Hailly (Ed.).—Une Campagne dans l'Océan Pacifique. (Febvrier Despointes). [Revue des Deux Mondes du 1" août 1858.]

Duhaut-Cilley.—Voyage autour du monde, principalement à la Californie et aux Iles Sandwich, pendant les années 1826–29. *Paris*, 1834–35. 2 vols. 8vo.

Duhaut-Cilley arrived at Honolulu the 17th of September, 1828, and left the 15th of November.

Dumont d'Urville (J. S. C.).—Philologie du Voyage de la Corvette *l'Astrolabe*, exécuté pendant les années 1826–29. *Paris*, Tastu, 1830. 1 vol. en 2 part. 8vo.

✗ —— Voyage pittoresque autour du monde. Résumé général des voyages de découvertes de Magellan, Bougainville, Cook, etc. *Paris*, 1834. 2 vols. 4to. Figs.

See Vol. I., pp. 406–476.

Du Petit-Thouars (Abel).—Voyage autour du monde sur la frégate *la Vénus*, éxécuté pendant les années 1838–39. *Paris*, Gide, 1841–49. 4 vols. 8vo, et atlas de 70 pl.

Du Petit-Thouars was at the Islands from the 10th to the 25th of July, 1837. He made a Treaty July 24th, in the name of Louis Phillipe, with Kamehameha III.

✗ Dwight (Rev. E. W.).—Memoirs of Henry Obookiah (Opukahaia). *New York*, 1832.

Dwight (Theodore).—Sketch of the Polynesian Language, drawn up from Hale's Ethnology and Philology. [Transactions of the American Ethnological Society. Vol. II.] *New York*, 1850.

Egerstrœm (C. Ax.)—Borta är bra, men hemma är bäst. *Söderköping*, 1859.

Travels in South America, California, Hawaiian Islands and Australia, 1852–57. Egerstrœm was three months at the Islands from March 29th, 1844.

Eichtal (G. d').—Mémoires sur l'Histoire primitive des Races Océaniennes et Américaines. *Paris*, 1843. 8vo.

—— Etudes sur l'Histoire primitive des Races Océaniennes et Américaines. *Paris*, 1845. 8vo.

This is simply the former work enlarged.

EKALESIA O TA HAKU, TA.—*Honolulu*, C. M., 1858. 8vo. pp. 16. B. (II. C.)

ELELE HAWAII.—Hawaiian Messenger. Edited by Rev. R. Armstrong (Limaikaika), from March 1845 to 1855.

ELLIS (W.).—Authentic Narrative of a Voyage performed by Capts. Cook and Clerke, during the years 1776–80. *London*, 1782. 8vo. (II. C.)

ELLIS (Rev. WILLIAM).—Narrative of a Tour through Hawaii or Owyhee; with Remarks on the History, Traditions, Manners, Customs and Language of the Inhabitants of the Sandwich Islands. *London*, 1826. 8vo. Map and woodcuts. A.

—— *Boston*, Crocker & Brewster, and *New York*, J. P. Haven, 1825. 12mo. pp. 264. Map and 5 pl. H. (II. C.)

—— Second Edition. ——

—— Polynesian Researches during a Residence of nearly six years in the Sandwich and Society Islands. *London*, 1829. 2 vols. 8vo. Illus.

—— Polynesian Researches during a Residence of nearly eight years in the Society and Hawaiian Islands. *London* and *New York*, Harpers, 1833. 12mo. pp. 1280. Illus. (II. C.)

—— Second Edition. *London*, 1853. 4 vols. 12mo. Figs. and maps.

—— Memoir of Mrs. Mary Mercy Ellis. *Boston*, 1856.

—— A Vindication of the South Sea Missions from the Misrepresentation of Otto von Kotzebue, with Appendix. *London*, 1831. 8vo.

—— On the burning Chasms of Ponohohoa, in Hawaii, one of the Sandwich Islands. [Brewster's Journal of Science (1st Series). Vol. V. p. 303.]

—— On the Volcano of Kilauea, Hawaii, one of the Sandwich Islands. [*Ibid.* Vol. VI. p. 151.]

—— The American Mission in the Sandwich Islands; a vindication and an appeal in relation to the proceedings of the Reformed Catholic Mission at Honolulu. *London*, 1866. 8vo. pp. 108.

EMERSON (Rev. J. S.).—Ai o ka la. Daily Food; with notes. *Honolulu*, M., 1835. 18mo. pp. 36.

—— 2d Edition, 1835. pp. 123. B. (II. C.)

—— Kumu mua, no na kamalii. *Honolulu*, M., 1837. 16mo. pp. 32. 3d Edition. B. (II. C.)

—— and BISHOP (Rev. A.).—He Hoakakaolelo no na hua olelo Beritania. *Lahainaluna*, 1845. B. (II. C.)

ENTERPRISE THE.—Edited by J. A. Thompson. Monthly. *Honolulu.*

ESCHSHOLTZ (FR.).—Zoologischer Atlas, enthaltend Abbildungen und Beschreibungen neuer Thierarten, während Kotzebue's zweiter Reise um die Welt, in den Jahren 1823–26, beobachtet. *Berlin*, Reimer, 1831. Fol. plates.

ETHNOGRAPHY.—See Coux, Crawford, Eichtal, Gobineau, Hale, Hollard, Lang, Meyen, Pickering, Quatrefages and Rae.

EYDOUX ET SOULEYET.—Zoologie du Voyage autour du monde de la Bonite, en 1836-37. *Paris*, Arthus Bertrand, 1841-52. 2 vols. 8vo, et atlas in fol. de 109 pl. coloriées.

EYRIÉS (J. B. B.).—See Broughton and Krusenstern.

✗ FANNING (Capt. EDM.).—Voyages round the world. *New York*, 1835. 8vo.

——— Voyage to the South Seas, Indian and Pacific Oceans, etc., with an account of the new discoveries in the Southern Hemisphere, between 1830 and 1832. 4th Ed. *New York*, 1838. 12mo.

FISCHER (Dr. ERN. L.).—See Langsdorff et Fischer.

FORBES (Rev. C.).—Ninau hoike. Doctrinal Catechism. *Honolulu*, M., 1841. 12mo. pp. 32. B.

FORSTER (R.).—See Anderson and Forster.

FORSTER (J. R.).—See La Pérouse.

· FRENCH TREATY, with the Report of the Committee of the Privy Council and the Protocols. *Honolulu*, 1858. 8vo.
Printed for the use of the Government.

✗ FREYCINET (LOUIS CLAUDE DE).—Voyage autour du monde, fait par ordre du Roi, sur les corvettes *l'Uranie* et *la Physicienne*, pendant les années 1817 à 1820. *Paris*, Pillet aîné, 1824-44. 3 vols. en 4 part. 4to, et Atlas fol. de 112 pl.
Freycinet was at the Islands in August 1819.

——— Navigation et Hydrographie (2 part). Figure du Globe et Observations du pendule. Magnétisme terrestre. Météorologie Ens. 5 part. 4to, et atlas fol. de 22 cartes.

FRIEND, THE.—A monthly Paper, edited by the Rev. S. C. Damon, D. D.; published since January, 1843. B. (H. C.)
Bimonthly in 1845–46–47; suspended from May to September, 1849, and from February, 1851, to May, 1852.

GAIMARD.—See Quoy et Gaimard.

GAIRDNER (MEREDITH).—Physico-Geognostic Sketch of the Island of Oahu, one of the Sandwich Islands. [Edinburgh New Philosophical Journal. Vol. XI., p. 1.—Hawaiian Spectator.]

——— Observations made during a Voyage from England to N. W. Coast of America. [*Ibid.* Vol. XVI.]

GALOPIN (CHARLES).—Notice sur les Iles Hawaii. *Geneva*, J. S. Fick, 1860. 8vo. (H. C.)

GAUSSIN (J. B.).—Du Dialecte de Tahiti, de celui des Iles Marquises et en général de la Langue Polynésienne. *Paris*, Didot, 1853. 8vo.

GAUDICHAUD.—Voyage autour du monde exécuté pendant les années 1817-20 sur *l'Uranie* et *la Physicienne*. Publ. par L. de Freycinet. Botanique. 4to. *Paris*, 1826. et Atlas de 120 pl.

—— Botanique du voyage autour du monde de la corvette *la Bonite* y compris la Cryptogamie par Montagne et Leveillé. 4 vols. 8vo. et Atlas de 156 planches in folio. *Paris*, Arthus Bertrand, 1840-66.

GEOGRAPHICAL SOCIETY, Journal of the Royal. *London*. See Vol. I., p. 193, 203;—IV., 258, 261, 333;—VI., 365, 440;—VII., 211, 221;—XII., 139;—XIII., 197.

GEOLOGY.—See Ball, Brigham, Chevalier, Coan, Couthouy, Dana, Darwin, Ellis, Gairdner, Goodrich, Green, Haldeman, Haskell, Hoffmann, Jackson, Kelly, Lyman, Mann, Parker, Stewart.

GERSTAECKER (F.).—Narrative of a Journey round the world, comprising a winter passage across the Andes to Chili, with a visit to the Gold Regions of California and Australia, the South Sea Islands, Java, etc. *New York*, 1854. 3 vols. 8vo.

GILL (WM.).—South Sea Islanders. *London*. 1 vol.

GOBINEAU (A. DE).—Essai sur l'inégalité des Races humaines. *Paris*, Didot, 1853-55. 4 vols. 8vo.

GOODRICH (Rev. JOSEPH).—On the volcanic character of the Island of Hawaii. [Silliman's Journal. Vol. XI. p. 1.]

—— Notices of some of the Volcanoes, and Volcanic Phenomena of Hawaii. [*Ibid*. Vol. XXV. p. 199.]

—— On some volcanic minerals. [*Ibid*. Vol. XVI. p. 345.]

GOULD (AUGUSTUS A.).—Mollusca and Shells of the United States Exploring Expedition. *Boston*. 4to. With folio Atlas.

GOULD (JOHN).—Description of a new species of the Genus Moho. M. apicalis. [Proceedings of the Zoölogical Society, 1860. p. 381.] [Annals of Natural History, Feb., 1861.] *London*, 8vo.

GRAY (ASA).—Botany of the United States Exploring Expedition. Phanerogamia. *New York*, 1854-57. 4to. With Atlas fol. 100 pl.

—— Descriptions of Hawaiian Plants in Proceedings of the American Academy of Arts and Sciences. Vol. IV., pp. 33-50; 306-324; V., pp. 115-152; 321-352; VI., pp. 37-55; 554.

GRAY (Dr. J. E.).— Description of three new species of Fish from the Sandwich Islands. [Zoölogical Miscellany, p. 33.]

GREEN (Rev. J. S.).—O ka la Sabati. *Lahainaluna*, 1835. 12mo. pp. 12.

—— Ka Mooolelo no ka Ekelesia o Iesu Kristo. Church History. *Lahainaluna*, 1835. 18mo. pp. 95. B. (H. C.)

—— 2d Edition. *Lahainaluna*, 1841. 12mo. pp. 340.

—— Mooolelo honua. Compendium of History. *Lahainaluna*, 1842. 12mo. pp. 76.

—— Notices of the Life, Character and Labors of the late Bartimeus L. Puaaike. *Lahainaluna*, 1844.

—— and CLARK (Rev. E. W.).—Notices of Bartimeus and Hawaii, two Christian Sandwich Islanders. *Boston*, Mass. Sabbath School Society, 1845. 18mo. pp. 126.

GREEN (WM. L.).—Geological Notices of the Sandwich Islands. [Sandwich Island Magazine, April, 1856.] *Honolulu*.

GREENHOW (ROBERT). — Memoir, Historical and Political, on the Northwest Coast of North America and the adjacent Territories. *Washington*, 1840. 8vo.

—— The History of Oregon and California, etc.; accompanied by a Geographical View and Map of those Countries, etc. *New York*, 1840. 8vo.

—— 3d Edit. *New York*, 1845. 8vo. Map.

GREGG (DAVID L.)—Oration delivered July 4th, 1854, at Honolulu. *Honolulu*, 1854. 8vo. H.

GULICK (L. H.).—New Testament Stories. In the Ponape Dialect. *Honolulu*, M., 1859. pp. 40.

—— Eight Chapters of Matthew. In the Ponape Dialect. *Honolulu*, 1859. pp. 20.

—— Bible Stories. In the Ponape Dialect. Reprint. *Honolulu*, 1865. pp. 61.

GULICK (Mrs. L. L.).—Tapi en Turapa. Primer in Ponape dialect. *Honolulu*, 1858. 12mo. pp. 36. B. (H. C.)

HAAWINA PALAPALA HEMOLELE, NA, NO KE KULA SABATI.—Bible Lessons. *Honolulu*, M., 1840. 12mo. pp. 83. Woodcuts. B. (H. C.)

HAE HAWAII.—The Hawaiian Flag. Edited by J. Fuller. From March 5th, 1856 to Dec., 1861.

HAE KIRITIANO.—The Christian Flag. Roman Catholic Mission. From Jan., 1850.

HAE HAVAII, NO TA.—*Honolulu*, C. M., 1858. 8vo. pp. 8. B. (H. C.)

HAIAO, NA.—Sermons by various authors. *Honolulu*, M., 1841. 12mo. pp. 296. (H. C.)

HAIMANAVA, no ta oihana katolika ma Havaii nei. *Honolulu*, C. M., 1858. 8vo. pp. 72. B. (H. C.)

HALDEMAN (S. S.).—On the Artificial Production of Capillary Lava. [Proceedings of the American Philosophical Society. Vol. IV. p. 5.) *Philadelphia.*

——— On Apus affinis, a new species from the Sandwich Islands. [Emmons American Journal, 1847.]

HALE (HORATIO).—Ethnography and Philology of the United States Exploring Expedition during the years 1838–42. *Philadelphia*, 1845. 4to. pp. xii. and 666. 3 maps.

——— Grammars and Vocabularies of all the Polynesian Languages. *Philadelphia*, 1846. 4to.

——— Migrations in the Pacific Ocean; from the volume on the Ethnography and Philology of the United States Exploring Expedition. *London*, 1846. 8vo. Maps.

HANDEL UND SCHIFFAHRT der Sandwich-Inseln von 1846 bis 1860. [Preuss. Handels-Archiv. 4 Oct. 1861.]

HASKELL (ROB. C.).—A visit to the recent Eruption of Mauna Loa, Hawaii. [Silliman's Journal. Vol. XXVIII (2). pp. 66–71.]

HAWAIIAN CASCADE AND MISCELLANY.—Monthly paper. From Nov. 1844 to Aug. 1845. Published by the Temperance Society. *Honolulu.*

HAWAIIAN EVANGELICAL ASSOCIATION.—Proceedings from June 3d to July 1st, 1863. *Boston*, Marvin & Son, 1864. 12mo. pp. 125. (H. C.)

HAWAIIAN GAZETTE.—Weekly paper, published by Government since Jan. 21st, 1865.

X HAWAIIAN CLUB PAPERS.—*Boston*, 1868. 8vo. pp. 119. B. (H. C.)

HAWAIIAN MATERNAL ASSOCIATION, Names of Members, and children of the. *Honolulu.*

This curious Pamphlet contains the names and ages of all the children born in the American Mission families.

HAWAIIAN MISSIONARY SOCIETY.—See Reports of.

HAWAIIAN SPECTATOR.—*Honolulu*, 1838–39. 2 vols. 8vo. I., pp. 440; II., pp. 494. B. (H. C.)

HELU KAMALII.—Mental Arithmetic from W. Fowle. *Honolulu*, 1859. 24mo.

HELUNAAU.—*Boston*, 1864. 16mo.

HENRICY (CASIMIR).—Histoire de l'Océanie depuis son origine jusqu'en 1846, suivie de notices biographiques sur ses grands hommes. *Paris*, Pagnerre, 1846. 8vo.

HENRY.—See Vancouver.

HERVAS (D. LORENZO).—Catalogo de las Lenguas de las Naciones conocidas, y Numeracion, Division, y Classes de estas segun la Diversidad de sus Idiomas y Dialectos. *Madrid*, 1800–1805. 6 vols. 4to. See Vol. II., Chap. I.

✗ HILL (S. II.).—Travels in the Sandwich and Society Islands. *London*, 1856. 8vo. (H. C.)

Hill remained on the Islands from January 29th to May 5th, 1849. See Revue des Deux Mondes, 15 Dec., 1856. Un Voyageur anglais aux Iles Sandwich, la civilisation dans l'Archipel, par M. Emile Montéqut.

HIMENI, NA MAU.—Hymn Book. 2d Ed. *Honolulu*, M., 1826. 8vo. pp. 60. Old orthography.

——— 5th Edition enlarged. *Honolulu*, M., 1830. 8vo. pp. 108.

HIMENI HOOLEA, NA.—He mau mele ma ka uhane. Hymns. *Honolulu*, M., 1839. 16mo. pp. 184.

——— 2d Edition, 1855. pp. 308.

——— 3d Edition, H. M. W., 1864. pp. 389. B. (H. C.)

HIMENI KAMALII, NA.—Children's Hymn-book. *Honolulu*, M., 1842, 16mo. pp. 101. B. (H. C.)

HIMENI HAWAII, NA, he me ori ia Iehova. Hymns. *Honolulu*, M. 1823. 24mo. pp. 60. Old orthography. B. (H. C.)

——— 2d Edition, 1826.

——— 5th Edition, 1830.

——— See Kumu Leomele, Kumu o ke Mele ano, Lira, etc.

HINDS (R. B.).—Zoölogy of the Voyage round the world of H. M. ship *Sulphur*, under Capt. Sir Edward Belcher, in 1836–42. *London*, 1843–45. 2 vols. 4to. pl.

⋋ HINES (Rev. GUST.)—Life on the Plains of the Pacific. Oregon; its History, etc., embracing extended Notes of a Voyage round the world. *Buffalo, N. Y.*, 1857. 8vo.

Hines was at the Islands from the 27th of February to April 3d, 1844.

HISTOIRE DES ILES SANDWICH et de la Mission Américaine, depuis 1820. Traduit de l'anglais. *Paris*, Risler, 1836. 18mo.

HISTORY.—See Anderson (R), Bingham, Cheever, Dibble, Ellis, Hopkins, Jarves, Remy, Simpson, Stewart, etc.

HOFFMANN (E.). — Observations géognostiques, faites pendant un Voyage autour du monde par O. de Kotzebue. [Karts Archiv. 1st Series. Vol. II.]

HOIKEMOLOHOLONA na na Kamalii, He. Stories about Animals. *Lahainaluna*, 1835.

HOIKE HONUA.—Geography. *Honolulu*, M., 1845. 12mo. Illus.

HOKU LOA.—Morning Star. Monthly paper. From July 2, 1859. *Honolulu*, M.

Hoku Loa Kalavina, no ka.—Monthly paper. From July to December, 1859. *Honolulu*, Roman Catholic Mission.

Hoku o ka Pakipika.—Star of the Pacific. Weekly paper. From Sept. 7, 1861.

Hollard (Dr. H.).—De l'Homme et des Races humaines. *Paris*, 1853. 12mo.

Honolulu Times.—A Weekly paper. Edited by H. L. Sheldon and Edw. C. Munn. From Nov., 1849 to July, 1851.

Hooiliili Havaii.—He mau hana, olelo, manao e pili ana o te Havaii nei. *Honolulu*, C. M., 1858. 8vo. pp. 8. B. (H. C.)

Hooker (W. Jackson) and Arnott (G. A. W.).—Botany of Capt. Beechey's Voyage, comprising an account of the Plants collected by Messrs. Say and Collie . . . . during the Voyage to the Pacific and Behring's Straits, performed under the command of Capt. Beechey. *London*, G. H. Bohn, 1831–40. 4to, and Atlas of 94 pl.

Hopkins (Manley).—Hawaii, the Past, Present and Future of its Island-Kingdom. An historical account of the Sandwich Islands (Polynesia). With a Preface, by the Bishop of Oxford. *London*, Longmans, 1862. 8vo. Map and woodcuts. pp. 423.

X ——— 2d Edition, revised and continued. *London*, 1866. 8vo.

For a Review, see Quarterly Review, XVII., pp. 219–236. (H. C.)

Hoppner (R. B.)—See Krusenstern.

Huinahelu.—Arithmetic. *Honolulu*, M., 1852. 12mo. (H. C.)

Huliano, O Ka.—He olelo niele ia a moakaka ai ke ano o ka Palapala Hemolele. Bible Questions. *Honolulu*, M, 1836. 18mo. pp. 155. 2d Ed. (H. C.)

Humboldt (Alex. von).—Essai politique sur le Royaume de la Nouvelle-Espagne. *Paris*, 1811. 4to. See p. 724.

Humboldt (Wm. von).—Ueber die Kawi-Sprache auf der Insel Java, nebst einer Einleitung über die Verschiedenheit des menschlichen Sprachbaues und ihren Einfluss auf die geistige Entwickelung des Menschengeschlechts. *Berlin*, 1836. 3 vols. 4to.

Hunt (Rev. T. Dwight).—Lectures. San Francisco.

Ike mua, o ka; he palapala ia e ao aku ai i na kamalii, etc. Reading Book. *Honolulu*, M., 1840. 12mo. pp. 48. (A. B. C. F. M.)

Iesu Kirito Evanelio Hemolelo e liko me to Mateo, To. unuhiia noloto mai a to Vulgate. *Honolulu*, C. M., 1853. 32mo. pp. 204. B. (H. C.)

ISLANDS OF THE PACIFIC.—[Quarterly Review, July 1859.]

ISLES SANDWICH, en 1853, Les. [Nouvelles Annales de la Marine. Avril 1859.]

JACKSON (Dr. CHAS. T.).—On specimens of Lava, presented to the Boston Society of Natural History by the American Board of Commissioners for Foreign Missions, from the Volcano Kilauea in Hawaii. [Proceedings of the Boston Society of Natural History, Vol. II, p. 120.] *Boston*, 1841. 8vo.

JACOBS (ALFRED).—Les Européens dans l'Océanie. Essai d'éducation morale et religieuse dans nos Colonies du Pacifique et les Isles Sandwich. [Revue des Deux Mondes, Sept. 1st, 1859.]

—— L'Océanie nouvelle, Colonies, Migrations, Mélanges. *Paris*, 1861, 12mo.

JARVES (JAMES JACKSON).—History of the Hawaiian or Sandwich Islands; embracing their Antiquities, Mythology, Legends, Discovery by Europeans in the 16th century, Re-discovery by Cook, with their Civil, Religious and Political History from the earliest traditionary period to the present time. *Boston*, Tappan & Dennett, 1843. 8vo. pp. 407. Map. Illus. B.

—— 3d Edition. *Honolulu*, C. E. Hitchcock, 1847. 8vo. pp. 240. Double columns. (H. C.)

—— Scenes and Scenery in the Sandwich Islands, and a Trip through Central America; being Observations from my Note Book during the years 1837–1842. *Boston*, Munroe & Co., 1843. 18mo. pp. 341. Map and figs. (H. C.)

—— 2d Edition. *Boston*, 1847.

—— Kiana, a tradition of Hawaii. *Boston*, 1857.

—— The Sandwich or Hawaiian Islands, with a Review of the past and present Condition of the Polynesian Groups generally, in connection with their Relations to Commerce and Christendom. [Hunt's Merchants' Magazine and Commercial Review. July, 1843.] *New York*.

JOHNSON (F.).—See Church Music.

JUDD (Dr. G. P.).—Anatomia. He palapala ia e hoike ai i ke ano o ke Kanaka kino. *Honolulu*, M., 1838. 12mo. pp. 60. 57 copperplates. B. (H. C.)

—— See Reports.

KAMEHAMEHA III.—His late Majesty Kauikeouli, Kaleiopapa, Kuakamanolani, Mahinalani, Kalaninuiwaiakua, Keaweawealaakalani, whose royal style was Kamehameha III. Obituary. *Honolulu*, by authority, 1854. Broadside. (H. C.)

KAMEHAMEHA IV.—Ka Buke o ka pule ana a me ka hooko ana i na kauoha hemolele, e like me ka mea i kauohaia no ka haipule ana ma ka pae aina Hawaii. Ua huiia hoi me na halelu a Davida, i hookaawaleia i mea e himeni ai a heluhelu ai paha iloko o na halepule. Book of Common Prayer, English, translated with a Preface by the King. *Honolulu*, 1862. 8vo. pp. 397.

——— Preface to the Book of Common Prayer, composed by the late King of Hawaii. *London*, 1866. 12mo. pp. 20.

——— Speeches. *Honolulu*, Government Press, 1861. 8vo. pp. 43. (H. C.)

KANAWAI O IEHOVA, KE.—Commandments of God. *Honolulu*, M., 1826. 8vo. pp. 4.

——— He olelo no na. *Honolulu*, M., 1834. 12mo. pp. 15. (A. B. C. F. M.)

——— Statute Laws of H. M. Kamehameha III. 1845–46; to which are appended the acts of public recognition, and the treaties with other nations. *Honolulu*, 1836. 8vo. 2 vols. In Hawaiian and English. B. (H.C.)

——— Statute Laws of 1847. *Honolulu*, 1847. 8vo. Hawaiian and English. B. A. (H.C.)

——— Statute Laws of H. M. Kamehameha III., 1851. *Honolulu*, 1851. 2 vols. 8vo. In Hawaiian and English. B. (H.C.)

——— HOOPAI KARAIMA. Criminal Code, 1850. *Honolulu*, 1852. 8vo. 2d Edition. B. (H.C.)

——— Statute Laws of H. M. Kamehameha III., 1853. *Honolulu*, 1853. 8vo. 2 vols. In Hawaiian and English. B. (H.C.)

——— Statute Laws of Kamehameha IV., 1855. *Honolulu*, 1855. 2 vols. 8vo. In Hawaiian and English. B. (H.C.)

——— ditto. 1856. B. (H.C.)

——— KIVILA. Civil Code of the Hawaiian Islands, passed in 1859, to which is added an Appendix containing other Laws, and Treaties with foreign nations. *Honolulu*, 1859. 2 vols. 8vo. In Hawaiian and English. B. (H.C.)

——— Statute Laws of H. M. Kamehameha IV., 1860. *Honolulu*, 1860. In Hawaiian and English. B. (H.C.)

——— ditto. 1862. B. (H.C.)

——— ditto. 1864–65. B. (H.C.)

KAUWAHI (J. W. H.).—KUHIKUHI O KANAKA HAWAII. Hawaiian Form Book. *Honolulu*, H. M. W., 1857. 8vo.

KEBLE (Rev. J.).—Seedtime and Harvest. Sermon preached at Hursley, Sept. 15th, 1864, at a Farewell Service to the Hawaiian Sisters. (For private circulation.) *London*, Lothian & Co., 1866. 8vo.

✗ KELLY (EDW. G.).—Remarks on the Geological features of Hawaii. [Silliman's Journal. Vol. XL., p. 117.] *New Haven*, Conn. Plate.

KEOPUOLANI, MEMOIR OF.—*Boston*, A. B. C. F. M., 1825. 12mo. pp. 48. (II. C.)

KUMU HAWAII.—Edited by Rev. Reuben Tinker. From Nov. 12th, 1834. *Honolulu*.

KUMU KAMALII, KE.—Lessons for Children. *Honolulu*. M. 1837. 16mo. pp. 144. Woodcuts and music. B. (II. C.)

KUMU KANAWAI, KE, etc.—*Honolulu*, 1840. 12mo. pp. 24. (A. B. C. F. M.)

——— KANAWAI, KE, a me na Kanawai o ko Hawaii poe aina. Constitution and Laws of H. M. Kamehameha III. *Honolulu*. 1841. 12mo. pp. 196. B. (H. C.)

——— ditto. 1852. In Hawaiian and English. B. (II. C.)

——— ditto. Constitution forced on to the people by H. M. Kamehameha V., by the force of circumstances, King of the Hawaiian Islands, on the twentieth day of August, 1864. *Honolulu*, 1864. 8vo.

——— LEOMELE, O KE. No na himeni, a me na halelu. Hymns and tunes. *Honolulu*, M., 1834. 16mo. pp. 360. B. (H. C.)

——— MUA ANA HOU. ABC Primer. *Boston*, O. Ellsworth, 1862. 12mo. illus. B. (II. C.)

——— MUA HOU. *New York*, Am. Tract Society. 16mo. illus. (II. C.)

——— O KE MELE ANO, O KE. Singing Book. Oblong 8vo. *Honolulu*, n. d. Music.

KING (Capt. JAMES).—See Cook.

✗ KIPPIS (ANDREW).—Life of Captain James Cook. *London*, 1788. 4to. Portrait by Heath.

——— Vie du capitaine Cook, traduit de l'anglais de Kippis, par Castera. *Paris*, 1789. 4to.

KITTLITZ (F. H. VON).—Beschreibung mehrerer neuer oder wenig gekannter Arten des Geschlechtes *Acanthurus* im Stillen Ocean. *Frankfort*, 1834. 8vo. 2 pl.

λ KITTLITZ (F. H. VON).—Twenty-four Views of the Vegetation of the Coasts and Islands of the Pacific, taken during the Exploring Voyage of the Russian Corvette *Seniawine*, Capt. Lütke, in the years 1827-29. *London*, 1861.

KOTZEBUE (OTTO VON).—Poutechestvie v ïoujenoï okéan. Voyage in the South Seas and Behring's Straits, in 1815-16-17-18 on the *Rurik* in search of the northeast passage. In Russian. *St. Petersburg*, Gretsch, 1821-23. 3 vols. 4to. Atlas fol.

KOTZEBUE (OTTO VON).—Reise in de Süd See und nach der Behring's Strasse, in den Jahren 1815-18. *Weimar*, Hoffmann, 1821. 3 vols. 4to. Figs. and maps.

—— English translation. *London*, Longman, 1821. 3 vols. 8vo. Figs. colored.

—— Dutch translation. *Amsterdam*, 1822.

.Kotzebue touched at Hawaii the 22d Nov., 1816; thence to Honolulu, where he remained until the 14th of December; returning September 27, 1817, he left October 14th.

—— Poutechestvie vokroug svéta. Voyage round the World, performed in the years 1823-26, on the sloop of war *Predprieatii*. In Russian. *St. Petersburg*, Press of the Marine, 1828. 8vo.

—— Reise um die Welt in den Jahren 1823-26. *St. Petersburg*, Brief, 1830. 2 vols. 8vo. With pl. and 8 maps.

—— Neue Reise um die Welt in dem Jahren 1823-26. *Weimar*, 1830. 2 vols. 8vo. Illus.

✗ —— English translation. *London*, 1830. 2 vols. 8vo.

KRUSENSTERN (A. J. VON).—Wörstersammlungen aus den Sprachen einiger Völker des östlichen Asiens und der Nordwest Küste von Amerika. Bekannt gemacht von A. J. von Krusenstern. *St. Petersburg*, 1813. 4to.

KRUSENSTERN (Capt. A. T. VON). — Poutechestvie vokroug svéta. Voyage round the world, performed in the years 1803-06, on the *Nadéjeda* and *Néva*. In Russian. *St. Petersburg*, 1809-12. 3 vols. 8vo. Atlas fol.

—— Reise um die Welt, in den Jahren 1803-1806. *St. Petersburg*, Imperial Press, 1810-12. 3 vols. 4to. Atlas fol. of 33 maps and 72 plates.

—— Abridgement in German. *Berlin*, 1811-12. 2 vols. 12mo. Illus.

—— Voyage round the World, 1803-06, on board the ships *Nadeshda* and *Neva*. Translated from the German by R. B. Hoppner. *London*, 1813. 2 vols. 4to. Illus.

—— Voyage autour du monde, fait dans les années 1803-06, sur les vaisseaux commandés par M. de Krusenstern, traduit, de l'aveu et avec les additions de l'auteur, par M. J. B. B. Eyriès. *Paris*, Gide fils, 1821. 2 vols. 8vo, et un atlas de 30 pl.

Krusenstern arrived at the Islands June 17th, 1804, and remained three days.

—— Memoir of Admiral John de Krusenstern, translated from the German by his daughter, Madame Charlotte Bernhardi, and edited by Adm. Sir John Ross. *London*, 1856. 8vo. Portr.

KRUSENSTERN (Capt. A. T. VON).—Recueil de Mémoires hydrographiques pour servir d'analyse et d'explication à l'atlas de l'Océan Pacifique. *St. Petersburg*, 1824-27-35. 3 pts. 4to, et atlas fol. de 34 cartes.

KUHIKUHI NO KA PALAPALA HEMOLELE, HE.—Buke I, II. *Lahainaluna*, 1839. 12mo. pp. 35. (2) B. (II. C.)

LAFOND DE LURCY (GABRIEL).—Voyages autour du monde et naufrages célèbres par le capitaine Gabriel Lafond de Lurcy. *Paris*, 1844-48. 8 vols. 8vo.
    Capt. Lafond visited the Islands in May, 1828. See Vol. IV., pp. 1-74.

LAHAINALUNA.—Laws of the High School, with a Catalogue. In Hawaiian and English. *Lahainaluna*, 1835. 12mo. pp. 28. B. (II. C.)

LAIEKAIWAI.—The Lady of the Twilight. A Hawaiian Romance. *Honolulu*, H. M. W. 12mo.

LAMA HAWAII.—A paper edited by Rev. L. Andrews. *Lahainaluna*, from Feb. 14 to Dec. 26, 1834. The first Journal published in the Pacific. The woodcuts were engraved by Dr. Alery Chapin of the American Mission at Lahaina. B. (II. C.)

LANG (JOHN DUNMORE).—View of the Origin and Migrations of the Polynesian Nation; demonstrating their ancient discovery and progressive settlement on the Continent of America. *London*, 1834. 12mo. pp. 256.

LANGSDORFF (GEO. HENRY VON).—Bemerkungen auf einer Reise um die Welt in den Jahren, 1803-07. *Frankfurt-am-Mein*, Wilmans, 1812. 2 vols. 4to. 40 pl.

—— Voyages and Travels in various parts of the world during the years 1803-07. *London*, 1813-14. 2 vols. 4to. Portrait and figs.

—— and FISCHER (FR. ERN. L.)—Plantes recueillies pendant le Voyage des Russes autour du monde, expédition dirigie par M. de Krusenstern; parties I. et II.; Icones Filicum. *Tubingen*, 1810-18. fol. de 36 pp. et 30 pl.

LA PÉROUSE (J. F. GALAUP DE).—Voyage autour du monde (pendant les années 1785-88) rédegé et publiée par M. L. A. Millet-Mureau. *Paris*, de l'Imprimerie de la République, an V (1797). 4 vol. 4to, et un atlas fol. de 70 pl.

—— 2d Edition. *Paris*, 1798. 3 vols. 8vo. A.

—— A Voyage round the world, 1785-88, under the command of John Francis Galaup de Lapérouse. Translated from the French. *London*, 1799. 2 vols. 4to. Atlas fol. 69 maps and figs.

—— 2d Edition. *London*, 1798. 2 vols. 8vo. Portr. and 51 figs.

LA PÉROUSE (J. F. GALAUP DE).—3d Edition. *London*, 1799. 3 vols. 8vo. and an atlas of maps and figs.

———— German translation, with notes by J. R. Forster and Chr. Sprengel. *Berlin*, 1799. 2 vols. 8vo.

———— Swedish translation by Samœdham. *Stockholm*, 1799. 8vo.

———— 4th English Edition. *London*, 1807. 3 vols. 8vo. and atlas.

———— Voyage de la Pérouse, rédigé d'après ses manuscrits originaux, suivi d'un appendice renfermant tout ce que l'on a découvert depuis le naufrage jusqu'à nos jours, et enrichi de notes par M. de Lesseps, seul débris vivant de l'expedition dout il était interprète. *Paris*, Arthus Bertrand, 1831. 8vo. With map, portrait and facsimile.

La Pérouse sighted Hawaii May 28th, 1786; arrived at Maui the 29th and left the 1st of June.

LAPLACE (CYR. P. THÉOD.).—Campagne de circumnavigation de la frégate *l'Artémise*, pendant les années 1837 à 1840. *Paris*, Arthus Bertrand, 1841, etc. 6 vols. 8vo. Fig. et cartes.

Laplace arrived the 9th and left on the 20th of July, 1839, after disgracing himself and his government, stealing twenty thousand dollars, and compelling the admission of brandy into the port, etc. See Hawaiian Spectator, Vol. II.; N. A. Review, No. 109; Castle, S. N.

LAURENT.—Zoophytologie du Voyage autour du monde de *la Bonite* en 1836–37. *Paris*, Arthus Bertrand, 1844. 8vo. et atlas de 6 pl.

LAW REPORTS.—Reports of some of the Judgments and Decisions of the Courts of Record of the Hawaiian Islands for the ten years ending with 1856. By George M. Robertson, pp. 328.— Reports of a portion of the Decisions rendered by the Supreme Court of the Hawaiian Islands, in Law, Equity, Admiralty and Probate, 1857–65. By Robert G. Davis. *Honolulu*, J. H. Black, 1857–66. 2 vols. 8vo. B. (H. C.)

LAWS.—See Kanawai, Kumukanawai.

LEBAS.—See Dixon.

LEDYARD.—The Life of John Ledyard, the American Traveller; comprising selection, from his Journals and Correspondence. *Cambridge, Mass*, 1828. 8vo. By Jared Sparks. B. (H. C.)

———— Memoirs of the life and travels of John Ledyard, from his Journal and Correspondence. By Jared Sparks. *London*, 1828. 8vo. (H. G.)

———— Travels and Adventures of John Ledyard, comprising his Voyage with Capt. Cook's third and last Expedition, etc. *London*, 1834. 8vo.

———— Life of John Ledyard, etc. *Boston*, 1847.

LEDYARD.—Journal, *Hartford, Conn.*, 1783.
> Ledyard was sergeant of infantry in Cook's third voyage. His Journal, written during the voyage, was seized by the Admiralty, but on his return to this country he re-wrote it, and it was published at Hartford.

LESSEPS.—See La Pérouse.

LICHTENSTEIN (H.)—Beitrag zur Ornithologischen Fauna, von Californien und über einige Vögel von den Sandwichs Inseln. [Abhandlungen Berliner Akademie, 1838, p. 417.] *Berlin*.

LIRA KATOLIKA.—Supplementum. *Honolulu*, C. M., 1864. 4to. oblong. pp. 40. B. (II. C.)

LIRA HAWAII.—He mau leomele no na Ekalesia O Hawaii nei. Church music. *Honolulu*, M., 1848. pp. 104. 2d Edition, 1855. 8vo. pp. 104. B. (II. C.)

LIRA KAMALII.—Songs and Tunes for the Sunday School. *New York*, Am. Tract. Soc., 1862. 16mo. pp. 192. B. (II. C.)

LISIANSKI (Capt. Lieut. JOURY). — Poutechestvīe vokroug svéta. Voyage around the world, performed in the *Néva*, in 1803–06. In Russian. *St. Petersburg*, Drechsler, 1812. 2 vols. 8vo, and fol. atlas.

✗ ——— Voyage round the world in the years 1803–06; performed by order of Alexander I., Emperor of Russia, in the ship *Néva*, by Urey Lisianski. *London*, Booth, 1814. 4to. Illus.

LŒWENSTERN (IS. DE).—See Voyages nouveaux par mer et par terre, effectués ou publiés de 1837 à 1847; pub. par Albert Montement. *Paris*, 1847. 5 vols. 8vo. Vol. I. p. 238.
> Lœwenstern was at the Islands three months at the beginning of 1839.

LUCETT.—Rovings in the Pacific, from 1837 to 1849; with a Glance at California, by a Merchant long resident at Tahiti. *London*, 1851. 2 vols.

LYMAN (Prof. C. S.).—Recent condition of Kilauea, 1852. [Silliman's Journal, Vol. XII. (2) pp. 75–80.]

LYMAN (Rev. D. B.)—No ka Wahahee. Tract on Lying. *Honolulu*, M., 1837. 12mo. pp. 8.

LYONS (Rev. L.)—Na himeni Kamalii. Children's Hymns. *Honolulu*, M., 1837. 24mo. pp. 72. B. (H. C.)

——— 2d Edition, 1838. pp. 122. B. (II. C.)

——— Na Haawina kamalii, no ke kula Sabati. Scripture Lessons. *Honolulu*, M., 1838. 12mo. pp. 152. 43 woodcuts. B. (H. C.)

MAILE QUARTERLY.—Published by the Hawaiian Mission Children's Society. *Honolulu*, H. M. W., from 1866. 8vo.

MANAO O NA ARII, KA.—Thoughts on Royalty. *Honolulu*, M., 1825. 18mo. pp. 8. Old orthography.

MANN (HORACE).—Denudation on the Hawaiian Islands. [Proceedings of the Boston Society of Natural History. Vol. X., p. 232.]
———— On some Hawaiian Crania and Bones. [*Ibid.* Vol. X. p. 229.]
———— Revision of the Genus Schiedea and some of the Rutaceæ. *Ibid.* Vol. X. pp. 309–319.]
———— On the present condition of Kilauea and Mauna Loa. [*Ibid.* Vol. X. p. 229.]
———— Description of the Crater of Haleakala. [*Ibid.* Vol. XI. p. 112.]
———— Enumeration of Hawaiian Plants. [Proceedings of the American Academy of Arts and Sciences. Vol. VII. pp. 143–235.]
———— Flora of the Hawaiian Islands. 8vo. In Press. [Proceedings of the Essex Institute. Vol. V.]

MANE LANI, O KA.—Ka ai na ka uhane. *Honolulu*, M., 1841. 18mo. pp. 69. B. (II. C.)

MANUALE NO TA POE KATOLIKA MA HAVAII.—*Honolulu*, C. M., 1857. 12mo. pp. 604, XL, X, 8. B. (II. C.)

A beautifully printed volume from the Catholic Press.

MAPS.—No topographical Surveys have been made. See Maps in Memoirs Boston Society of Natural History. Vol. I, pt. 3.

✗ MARCHAND (ETIENNE).—Voyage autour du monde, pendant les années 1790–92, précédé d'une introduction historique, etc., par C. P. Claret Fleurieu. *Paris*, Impr. de la République an VI–VIII (1798–1800). 4 vols. 4to. Figs.
———— 2d Edition. *Paris*, 1798–1800. 5 vols. 8vo. et atlas 4to.
———— A Voyage round the World, 1790–92, by Stephen Marchand. Preceded by an historical introduction, etc. *London*, 1801. 2 vols. 4to. and atlas.
———— Neueste Reise um die Welt. *Leipzig*, Hénrichs. 2 vols. 8vo.

Marchand made the south point of Hawaii October 5th, 1791, and arrived at Kauai on the 7th. Did not anchor.

MARINER (W.)—Account of the Natives of the Tonga Islands, with an original Grammar, etc., compiled and arranged from the extensive communications of W. Mariner, by John Martin. *London*, 1818. 2 vols. 8vo. Map and portr.

Mariner touched at the Islands in September, 1806, on the ship *Port au Prince*.

MARSDEN (WILLIAM).—Miscellaneous Works.—On the Polynesian or East Insular Languages. *London*, 1834. 4to. Maps and cuts.

MARTIN (JOHN).—See Mariner.

MARSHALL (JAMES F. B.)—Address at the Annual Meeting of the
Royal Hawaiian Agricultural Society, October 22d, 1857.
Honolulu. Roy. 8vo. pp. 8.

———— See Church Music.

MARTIN (WILLIAM).—Catalogue d'Ouvrages relatifs aux Iles Hawaii,
Essai de Bibliographie Hawaiienne. *Paris*, Challamel aîné.
1867. 12mo. pp. 92. B.

———— Notice sur les îles Hawaii; Exposition universelle de 1867 à Paris.
Paris, P. Dupont, 1868. 8vo. pp. 21. (II. C.)

MATHISON (G. F.).—Narrative of a visit to Brazil, Chili, Peru and the
Sandwich Islands, during the years 1821-22. With miscellaneous remarks on the past and present state, and political prospects of those countries. *London*, 1825. 8vo.

MEARES (JOHN).—Voyages made in the years 1788 and 1789, from
China to the Northwest coast of America; to which are prefixed an introductory narrative of a voyage performed in 1786, from Bengal, etc. *London*, 1790. 4to. Illus.

———— 2d Edition, 1791. 2 vols. 8vo. Illus.

———— 3d Edition, 1796.

———— French translation by Billecocq. *Paris*, an III (1795). 3 vols.
8vo, et un atlas 4to.

MEYEN (Dr. F. J. F.).—Beiträge zur Zoologie, gesammelt auf einer
Reise um die Erde. Dritte Abhandlung, Menscher-Raçen.
Breslau et Bonn, 1834. 4to. 41 pl. plain and colored.

———— Reise um die Erde, Aus gefuhrt auf dem Königlich Preussischen
Seehandlungs Schiffe *Princess Louisa*, commandirt von Capitain W. Wendt, in den Jahren 1830-32. *Berlin*, 1834-35.
2 vols. 4to.

MILLET-MUREAU (L. A.).—See La Pérouse.

MISSION AT THE SANDWICH ISLANDS.—[Christian Examiner, 1835.]
Boston.

———— Report on the Hawaiian Church Mission (Reformed Catholic).
London, 1866.

MISSIONARIES.—Instructions of the Prudential Committee to the several
Reinforcements sent out to the Sandwich Islands Mission.
Boston.

———— Comments on the Course of Missionaries in the Sandwich
Islands. [Edinburgh Review, Jan. 1844.]

———— American Missionaries at the Sandwich Islands. Refutation of
the Charges brought against them by the Roman Catholics.
Boston, 1841.

MISSIONARIES.—Answers to Questions proposed by H. Ex. R. C. Wyllie, Minister of Foreign Relations, and addressed to all the Missionaries in the Hawaiian Islands, May, 1846. *Honolulu*, 1848. 8vo.

MISSIONARY'S DAUGHTER, THE.—*New York*, 1841.

MISSIONARY GAZETTEER, comprising a View of the Inhabitants, and the Geographical Description of the Countries and Races where the Protestant Missionaries have labored. *Woodstock*, 1825.

MISSIONARY HERALD. (In 1868 this work consists of sixty-three vols., 8vo, forty-eight of which contain numerous, though generally brief, articles respecting the Islands. The entire collection relates to religious affairs, full index to which is not practicable in this book. Leading subjects are enumerated sufficiently to indicate the great amount of information on Hawaii contained in these volumes.) A. (H. C.)

Mission to the Islands announced, Vol. 15 (1819), p. 428; Ordination of Missionaries and formation of Mission church, do., p. 527; Embarkation of Missionaries, do., p. 528; Donations to, do., p. 567; Report of Prudential Committee respecting, do., p. 558; "Thaddeus" spoken, Vol. 16, p. 48; Description of arrival first missionaries, Vol. 17 (1821), pp. 111-122; Destruction of Idols, do.; p. 122.

Annual Review of Mission. Vol. 16 (1820), p. 48; Vol. 20 (1824), pp. 3, 4; Vol. 21 (1825), pp. 4, 211; Vol. 22 (1826), p. 4; Vol. 23 (1827), pp. 10, 211; Vol. 24 (1828), p. 7; Vol. 25 (1829), p. 9; Vol. 26 (1830), pp. 9, 310-19; Vol. 27 (1831), pp. 7, 118-22, 144-6, 152; Vol. 28 (1832), p. 5; Vol. 29 (1833), p. 19; Vol. 30 (1834), pp. 3, 367; Vol. 31 (1835), pp. 150, 17; Vol. 32 (1836), pp. 102-6, 17-19; Vol. 33 (1837), pp. 17, 273-81, 429, 475; Vol. 34 (1838), p. 10, and many more; Vol. 35 (1839), pp. 11, 141 et seq; Vol. 36 (1840), pp. 12, 222-7; Vol. 37 (1841), pp. 12, 145-53; Vol. 38 (1842), pp. 4, 9, 94, 461, 470; Vol. 39 (1843), p. 11; Vol. 40 (1844), pp. 8, 14-23, 118; Vol. 41 (1845), pp. 10, 69, 73-87; Vol. 42 (1846), pp. 11, 150-354; Vol. 43 (1847), pp. 11, 217-24; Vol. 44 (1848), pp. 10, 181-94; Vol. 45 (1849), pp. 11, 73-88; Vol. 46 (1850), pp. 12, 397-408; Vol. 47 (1851), pp. 11, 397-402; Vol. 48 (1852), pp. 10, 321-26, 335-7; Vol. 49 (1853), pp. 10, 369-79; Vol. 50 (1854), pp. 10, 11; Vol. 51 (1855), pp. 10, 11; Vol. 52 (1856), pp. 10, 11; Vol. 53 (1857), pp. 10, 11; Vol. 54 (1858), pp. 9, 10; Vol. 55 (1859), pp. 9, 10; Vol. 56 (1860), pp. 10, 11; Vol. 57 (1861), pp. 10, 11; Vol. 58 (1862), p. 15; Vol. 59 (1863), p. 9; Vol. 60 (1864), p. 10; Vol. 61 (1865), pp. 9, 10; Vol. 62 (1866), pp. 10, 11; Vol. 63 (1867), p. 9.

Mission : Condition of, reviewed, 1828, Vol. 25, p. 117; do. general, Vol. 30 (1834), p. 367, etc; Vol. 32, p. 305; Vol. 41 (1845), pp. 78, 358; Vol. 35 (1839), p. 482. Expense of, 1823, Vol. 20, p. 375. Episcopalian view of, Vol. 63, pp. 225-31. Foreign opposition to, Vol. 23 (1827), p. 202. Good done by, testimony, Vol. 42 (1846), pp. 145, 147; Vol. 56, 214. Journal of, see below. Missionaries, circular letter of, 1826, Vol. 23, p. 240. Reinforcements, contemplated, Vol. 17 (1821), 396; embarkation

of same, Vol. 19, pp. 11, 106; do. arrive, Vol. 20 (1824), pp. 179-81, 209; again contemplated, Vol. 23, pp. 227, 293, 325; do. arrive, Vol. 25 (1829), p. 20; again proposed, Vol. 26, pp. 334, 366; arrive, Vol. 28 (1832), pp. 74, 114; proposed, Vol. 31, (1835), pp. 18, 32, 281; do. arrive, Vol. 32 (1836), p. 81; do. Vol. 44 (1848), p. 367. Success of, prospect of, Vol. 20, (1824), pp. 111, 318; do. estimated 1833, Vol. 29, p. 453.
Missionary Society, Hawaiian, Vol. 50 (1854,) Vol. 48, p. 326.
Evangelical Association, Hawaiian, Annual retrospects of mission work, statistics, etc., Vol. 50 (1854), pp. 337-41; Vol. 51 (1855), pp. 321-23; Vol. 52 (1856), pp. 310-12; Vol. 53 (1857), pp. 337-40; Vol. 54 (1858), pp. 329-37; Vol. 55 (1859), pp. 292-94; Vol. 56 (1860), pp. 292-300; Vol. 57 (1861), pp. 291-95; Vol. 58 (1862), pp. 307-9; Vol. 59 (1863), pp. 256-99; Vol. 60 (1864), pp. 351-3; Vol. 61 (1865), pp. 293, 363-4; Vol. 62 (1866), p. 296; Vol. 63 (1867), 368-9.
Evangelical Association, Hilo, organized, Vol. 57 (1861), p. 67.
Mission to Marquesas, begun, Vol. 49 (1853), pp. 284, 373-5.

MISCELLANEOUS.

Alphabet, Vol. 19, p. 42; Annual meeting of Missionaries (last) with review for twenty-five years past, Vol. 49 (1853), p. 370. **Anderson,** Rev. Dr., on visit to Islands, Vol. 59 (1863), pp. 193-7. **American** affairs, Interest in, Vol. 60 (1864), p. 152. **Bible,** edition of, Vol. 40 (1844), p. 104, etc. **Bingham,** Rev. H. (early letters from) on board "Thaddeus," Vol. 16, p. 91; Vol. 17, p. 215; Vol. 18, p. 320; do. Journal at Atooi, Vol. 18, pp. 241-49. **Church** at Honolulu (first), Vol. 18 (1822), p. 92; new do. at do., Vol. 24 (1825), p. 248; Vol. 26, pp. 105, 280. **Clark,** on advance in ten years, Vol. 54 (1858), p. 335. **Coan,** Rev. T. (review of twenty years), Vol. 51 (1855), pp. 323-26; Vol. 52, p. 59; Vol. 60, pp. 73-5, 151, 298. **Tour** in Puna and Hilo, Vol. 61 (1865), pp. 134-7; do. do. Vol. 62, p. 42. **Communicants,** number in 1843, Vol. 40, pp. 9, 17, 48, 186. **Dana,** R. H. Jr., opinion on Mission, Vol. 56, pp. 214-16; **Foreign** aggression, Vol. 40 (1844), Vol. 47, etc. **Graham,** Mrs., corrected, Vol. 23, p. 271. **General** Intelligence (earlier years), Vol. 18 (1822), pp. 63, 65, 67, 90-2, 145, 189-91, 213, 241-50, 399; Vol. 19 (1823), pp. 11, 40, 96, 105, 205, 270; (reference to each volume may be made under this head). **Hopoo,** Thomas, letters, Vol. 18, pp. 146-7, 190. **Hawaii,** tour of, 1825, Vol. 23, pp. 48-55, 184. **Hilo,** school at, Vol. 40, pp. 9, 16; Vol. 45, pp. 42, 186. **Idolatry,** remains of, Vol. 24 (1828), p. 106; Vol. 27 (1831), p. 145; Vol. 30, p. 407. **Independence,** recognition of, Vol. 39 (1843), pp. 90, 131; Vol. 40, p. 10. **Influence**—of California, Vol. 46 (1850), p. 248; do. of Government, Vol. 31 (1835), p. 466. **Journal** of Mission, Vol. 17 (1821), pp. 169-178, 131-142, 241-50; Vol. 18 (1822), pp. 201-14, 320-24, (at Oahu) 273-80; Vol. 19, pp. 38-44, 97-105, 182-85, 281-3, 314-20, 350-2; Vol. 20, pp. 208-10, 245-48, 281-3, 315-18; Vol. 21, 172-4, 210-12, 248-50, 274-5; Vol. 22 (1826), 14-19, 40, 68-73, 108, 205-9, 369-72. **Kamehameha,** letters from, Vol. 19 (1823), p. 316; [See Reho Reho]; do. III., death of, Vol. 51 (1855). **Kekela,** Rev. J., Vol. 46, p. 406; Vol. 47, p. 400. **Kohala,** history of Station at, Vol. 41 (1845), pp. 79-83. **Lahaina,** Messrs. Stewart and Richards at, Vol. 21 (1825), pp. 39, 69, 212,

275; Vol. 22 (1826), pp. 36, 142-49, 169-76, 239-45; Vol. 23, pp. 38, 142: do., view of the **Meeting-House,** Vol. 35 (1839), 304. **Lahainaluna,** view of seminary, Vol. 35 (1839), p. 257; information on Schools, 1837, Vol. 34, p. 252; Vol. 35 (1839), p. 257; Vol. 40, pp. 9, 15; Vol. 41, pp. 10, 28, 76; Vol. 42, p. 419; Vol. 59, pp. 341, 298; Seminary burned, Vol. 58 (1862), p. 375. **Laws,** abstract of, Vol. 36 (1840), p. 101. **Loomis, E.,** letter from (first), Vol. 17, p. 215. **Map** of Islands, Vol. 28 (1832). **Maui,** population 1828, Vol. 25, p. 211; census, Vol. 28 (1832), p. 251; Vol. 44 (1847), p. 103. **Marriage,** prevalence of Christian form of, Vol. 26 (1830), p. 312; Vol. 28 (1832), p. 74; Vol. 29, p. 162. **Native ministry.** Ordination of first native minister, Vol. 46 (1850), p. 406; in general, see Vol. 61 (1865), p. 262; Vol. 62, p. 16; Vol. 63, pp. 47, 401. **Newspaper** (religious) attempted, 1834, Vol. 31, p. 149. **Paris,** Rev., statistics, etc., Vol. 54, p. 202. **Pele,** a pretended, Vol. 22 (1826), pp. 241-3. **People, condition of the,** Vol. 19 (1823), pp. 103, 183; Vol. 20 (1824), p. 112; Vol. 21 (1825), pp. 210-11; Vol. 22 (1826), pp. 42, 308; Vol. 23 (1827), pp. 55, 206; Vol. 25 (1829), pp. 183, 315; Vol. 26 (1830), pp. 10, 18, 107; Vol. 28 (1832), p. 155; Vol. 30 (1834), pp. 286, 368, 371, 341, 449; Vol. 34 (1838), p. 255; Vol. 35 (1839), pp. 146, 167, 258; Vol. 37 (1841), pp. 152, 147; Vol. 38 (1842), pp. 149, 156; Vol. 36 (1840), p. 222; Vol. 40 (1844), pp. 9, 17. 176, 188, 192; Vol. 39 (1843), p. 54, etc; Vol. 43 (1847), pp. 97, 219, 361; Vol. 46 (1850), pp. 402-8; Vol. 48 (1852), pp. 11, 161, 322, 324-6; Vol. 49 (1853), pp. 289, 377; Vol. 51 (1855), pp. 166, 322-5; Vol. 55 (1859), pp. 258-9, 293; Vol. 56 (1860), pp. 293, 297; Vol. 57 (1861), p. 250; Vol. 58 (1862), p. 374; Vol. 59 (1863), p. 112; Vol. 60 (1864), pp. 297, 352; Vol. 61 (1865), p. 364; Vol. 62 (1866), p. 17. **Press and Printing,** Vol. 20 (1824), p. 183; Vol. 21 (1825), p. 105; Vol. 22 (1826), p. 141; Vol. 24 (1828), pp. 8, 103, 210; Vol. 25 (1829), pp. 9, 26, 182, 262, 275, 397; Vol. 26 (1830), pp. 9, 19, 311, 316; Vol. 27 (1831), pp. 7, 117, 144; Vol. 28 (1832), pp. 6, 73; Vol. 29 (1833), pp. 16, 221, 456; Vol. 30 (1834), pp. 256, 283; Vol. 31 (1835), pp. 19, 147; Vol. 32 (1836), pp. 102, 317, 353; Vol. 34 (1838), p. 253; Vol. 35 (1839), pp. 145, 162; Vol. 36 (1840), p. 222; Vol. 37 (1841), p. 145; Vol. 40 (1844), p. 104. View of printing-office, Honolulu, Vol. 36 (1840), p. 223. **Population and Census,** Vol. 28 (1832), (Maui,) p. 251; ———— Islands, p. 22; Vol. 30 (1834), ———— p. 6; Vol. 32 (1836), ———— p. 305; Vol. 44 (1848), (Maui,) p. 103; Vol. 46 (1850), pp. 140, 397; Vol. 47 (1851), p. 12; Vol. 63 (1867), p. 215. Decrease of population, Vol. 43 (1847), pp. 93, 103, 220; Vol. 45 (1849), p. 74; Vol. 46 (1850), pp. 106-7, 397. **Poetry,** native, remarks on, Vol. 25, p. 372. **Reho Reho** (Kamehameha II.), visit to Europe and U. S. A., Vol. 20 (1824), p. 248; Vol. 21, p. 172; return of remains per "Blonde" Vol. 22, pp. 109, 172. **Rising,** F. S., view of Mission, Vol. 63, p. 225. **Romanism** (many references through work), see Vol. 28, p. 351; Vols. 40, 42, 45, 88. **Ruggles,** S., early letters from, Vol. 17, pp. 123, 216; Vol. 18, pp. 189, 321, etc. **School,** plan of High, for teachers, Vol. 28 (1832), pp. 188, 222. See Lahainaluna, Hilo, Wailuku, etc., and annual reports. In earlier years, Vol. 28 (1832), pp. 5, 72, 251; Vol. 29, pp. 267, 457; Vol. 30, pp. 257-448. **Sea,** remarkable rise and fall of, Vol. 34, pp. 244, 475. **Temperance** Society (general), formation of, Vol. 28 (1832), p. 115. **Ta-**

moree (King), letters from, Vol. 17 (1821), pp. 124, 142. **Tapoolee** (Queen), letters from, Vol. 17, pp. 124, 143. **Thurston,** A., letter from, Vol. 18, p. 190 (and many after). **Treaties** with England and France, Vol. 43 (1847), pp. 140-1. **Tornado** (Lahaina), Vol. 54, p. 335. **Volcanoes,** Vol. 39 (1843), pp. 381, 463; Vol. 37, p. 283; Vol. 40, p. 189; Vol. 48, pp. 225, 356; Vol. 52, p. 59. **Whitney,** S., letters from (earlier dates), Vol. 17 (1821), pp. 123, 216; Vol. 18, pp. 189, 321; Vol 19, p. 44, et seq. **Waialua** (new station at), Vol. 29 (1833), p. 365; (school at), Vol. 62 (1866), p. 197; Vol. 63, p. 211. **Wailuku,** Vol. 28 (1832), p. 250; Vol. 42, p. 188; Female boarding-school at, Vol. 40, pp. 9, 15. **Waimea,** Vol. 28, pp. 116, 222, 329, etc.

MISSIONARY RECORDS.—*London*, Religious Tract Society, 1840, etc.

—— Reports of the Hawaiian Missionary Society, presented by the Board of Directors. Annual. *Honolulu.* 12mo. Twelfth and Last Report, 1863. B. (H. C.)

MISSIONS.—Proceedings of the A. B. C. F. M., in relation to a recent interference with its work on the Sandwich Islands. *Boston*, 1865. 8vo. pp. 16.

MONITOR, THE.—Edited by Rev. Daniel Dole. Monthly paper for children. *Honolulu,* 1845.

MONTAGNE.—See Gaudichaud et Montagne.

MONTGOMERY.—See Tyerman and Bennett.

—— (JAMES).—Journal of Voyages and Travels. *Boston,* 1832. 8vo. (H. C.)

MOO-ATUA, TA; a me na taao o ta honua nei. *Honolulu,* C. M., 1858. 8vo. pp. 20. B. (H. C.)

MOOOLELO HAWAII.—Hawaiian History. *Lahainaluna,* 1838. 8vo.

By the Pupils in the Seminary of the American Mission. A portion was translated in the "Hawaiian Spectator," Jan., 1839.

—— 2d Edition, enlarged. Edited by Rev. J. F. Pogue. *Honolulu,* 1858. 8vo. pp. 86.

—— Ka Mooolelo Hawaii. See Rémy, Jules.

MOOOLELO NO KA EKALESIA.O IESU CHRISTO.— Church History. *New York,* 1863. 8vo. Illus.

MORELLET.—See Vancouver.

MOREMONA, KA BUKE A.—The Book of Mormon. *San Francisco.* 8vo. B. (H. C.)

✗ MORRELL (Capt. BENJ.).—Narrative of four voyages to the South Sea, North and South Pacific Ocean, etc., 1822-31. Comprising Critical Surveys of Coasts and Islands, with sailing Directions, etc., to which is prefixed a brief sketch of the author's early life. *New York,* 1832. 8vo. Port.

Morrell arrived at the Islands June 22d, 1825, and remained a week.

MORTIMER (Lieut. GEORGE).—Observations and Remarks made during a voyage to the Islands of Teneriffe . . . . Otaheite, Sandwich Islands, etc., in the brig *Mercury*, Commander John Henry Cox. London, 1791. 4to.

MOSBLECH (l'abbé BONIFACE). — Vocabulaire Océanien-Français et Français-Océanien des dialectes partés aux iles Marquises, Sandwich, Gambier, etc. *Paris*, J. Renouard, 1843. 12mo.

NONANONA.—The Ant. Edited by Rev. R. Armstrong. From the 6th of July, 1841, to March 18th, 1845. *Honolulu*.

NUHOU.—The News. Edited by James W. Marsh. March 10th, 1854. *Honolulu*.

NUPEPA KUOKOA.—Independent Press. Weekly since January, 1861. *Honolulu*, Dr. L. H. Gulick, Editor.

OAHU, and its Agricultural Prospects. [Nautical Magazine, 1856.]
——— COLLEGE. Catalogue of the Teachers and Pupils of Punahou School and Oahu College for Twenty-five years, ending 1866, with an account of the Quarter Century Celebration held at Punahou, June 15th, 1866. *Honolulu*, H. M. W., 1866. 8vo. pp. 49. B.
——— ——— at the Sandwich Islands. *Boston*, T. R. Marvin, 1856. 12mo. pp. 12. B. (H. C.)
——— FOUNTAIN.—A Monthly Temperance Journal. Edited by J. Peacock. From Jan. to Oct., 1847. B. (H. C.)

OLELO O KE AKUA, HE.—*Honolulu*, 1825. 8vo. pp. 4. Old orthography.

OLELO HOONAAU AO, HE.—Catechism of the Roman Catholic Mission. *Macao*, 1831. 8vo. pp. 48.

OLMSTEAD (FR. ALLYN).—Incidents of a Whaling Voyage; to which are added Observations on the Scenery, Manners and Customs, and Missionary Stations of the Sandwich and Society Isllands. Accompanied by numerous lithographic prints. *New York*, 1841. 12mo. Illus.

ORME (W.).—A Defence of the Missions in the South Seas and Sandwich Islands, against the Misrepresentations contained in a late number of the Quarterly Review. *London*, 1827.

ORNITHOLOGY.—See Cassin, Dole (S. B.), Eschscholtz, Eydoux et Souleyet, Gould (J.), Hinds, Lichtenstein, Peale, Quoy et Gaimard, Stanley, Vigors.

PACIFIC COMMERCIAL ADVERTISER. — Edited by H. M. Whitney. Weekly from July, 1856.

PACIFIC OCEAN, considered with reference to the Wants of Seamen. [Nautical Magazine, 1856.]

PALACE, Investigation at the, by command of the King, etc., with supplement and Appendix. *Honolulu*, 1847. 2 vols. 8vo. H.

PALAPALA HIMENI, no na Halepule a me na Halekula Katolika o Havaii. *Honolulu*, C. M., 1852. 18mo. pp. 140. Music 96, 10. B. (II. C.)

PALAPALA HOAKAKA i ke ano ino o na mea ona.—On the use of Intoxicating Drinks. *Honolulu*, M., 1837. 12mo. pp. 27. B. (H. C.)

PAPAINOA O KE KULANUI O LAHAINALUNA.—Catalogue of the High School at Lahainaluna. *Honolulu*, M. 1846. 8vo. pp. 14. B. (H. C.)

PAPA KUHIKUHI O NA KULIANA A PAU MA KA MOKUPUNI O OAHU.— Index of all the claims awarded on the Island of Oahu by the Land Commission. *Honolulu*, 1861. 8vo.

PARKER (Mrs. E. M. W.).— The Sandwich Islands as they are, not as they should be. *San Francisco*, 1852.

PARKER (Capt.).—On the Volcano of Kilauea with Plate. [Silliman's Journal. Vol. XL., p. 117.]

PARKHURST (JOHN L.).—Latin Lessons for Hawaiian Children. *Lahainaluna*, 1839. 18mo. pp. 32. B. (H. C.)

✓ PAULDING (HIRAM).—Journal of a cruise of the U. S. schooner *Dolphin*, among the Islands of the Pacific Ocean, etc. *New York*, 1831. 12mo. pp. 258. Map. A.

PEABODY (Rev. A. P.).—The Hawaiian Islands as developed by Missionary Labors. [Boston Review, May, 1865.] 8vo. pp. 24. B. (H. C.)

PEALE (TITIAN R.).—Mammalia and Ornithology of the United States Exploring Expedition. *Philadelphia*, 1848. 4to. (Suppressed.)

PEASE (W. HARPER).—A Catalogue of Works relating to the Hawaiian or Sandwich Islands. *Honolulu*, H. M. Whitney, 1862. 8vo. pp. 24. B.

—— Descriptions of New Species of Mollusca from the Sandwich Islands. [Proceedings of the Zoological Society, 1860. pp. 18, 141.] *London*.

—— Descriptions of New Species of Planariidæ collected in the Sandwich Islands. [*Ibid*. p. 37.]

—— Descriptions of seventeen New Species of marine shells from the Sandwich Islands. [*Ibid*. p. 397.]

—— Descriptions of forty-seven New Species of shells from the Sandwich Islands. [*Ibid*. p. 431.]

—— New Mollusca from the Sandwich Islands. [*Ibid*. 1861. p. 242.]

PEASE (W. HARPER).—Descriptions of two New Species of Helicter (*Achatinella*) from the Sandwich Islands, with a History of the Genus. [*Ibid.* 1862. p. 3.]
—— Marine Shells. [*Ibid.* p. 240.]
—— New Species of Shells from the Pacific Islands. [*Ibid.* p. 243.]
—— Marine Shells. [*Ibid.* p. 278.]
—— Additions, etc. [*Ibid.* 1863. p. 510.]

PERIODICALS published at the Islands. Those no longer issued (1868) are marked *.

AMERICAN.		HAWAIIAN.	
* Sandwich Island Gazette,	1836–39	* Lama Hawaii,	1834
* Hawaiian Spectator,	1838–39	* Kumu Hawaii,	1834
* Sandwich Island Mirror,	1839	* Nonanona,	1841–45
* Polynesian,	1840–62	* Elele Hawaii,	1845–55
Friend,	1843	* Nuhou,	1854
* Hawaiian Cascade and Miscellany,	1844–45	* Hae Hawaii,	1856–61
		* Hoku Loa,	1854
* Monitor,	1845	* No ka Hoku Loa Kalavina,	1859
* Oahu Fountain,	1847		
* Sandwich Island News	1846–47	* Hae Kiritiano,	1850
* Honolulu Times,	1844–51	* Hoku o ka Pakipika,	1861
* Transactions of the Royal Hawaiian Agricultural Society,	1850–56	Nupepa Kuokoa,	1861
		Au Okoa,	1865
		Alaula,	1866
* Weekly Argus,	1852–53		
* Amateur,	1852		
* New Era and Weekly Argus,	1853–55		
* Sandwich Island Monthly Magazine,	1856		
Pacific Commercial Advertiser,	1856		
Hawaiian Gazette,	1865		
* Daily Hawaiian Herald,	1866		

PERKINS (EDWARD T.).—Na Motu, or Reef Rovings in the South Seas, a Narrative of Adventures at the Hawaiian, Georgian and Society Islands, with Maps and an Appendix, relating to the Resources, Social and Political Condition of Polynesia, and Subjects of Interest in the Pacific. *New York*, 1854. 8vo. pp. 456. Illus. A.

PERREY (ALEXIS).—See his various annual catalogues of earthquakes since 1843. 8vo.

PETERMANN (AUG.).—Mittheilungen aus Justus Perthes Geographischer Anstalt, etc. See 1859, p. 188; 1861, p. 82.

PHILOLOGY.—See Alexander, Andrews, Bishop, Bopp, Chamisso, Crawfurd, Dumont d'Urville, Dwight, Gaussin, Hale, Hervas, Humboldt, Krusenstern, Marsden, Mosblech, Rae, Threlkeld.

PI-A-PA.—Primer. 18mo. pp. 12. n. d. (A. B. C. F. M.)

PICKERING (Dr. CHAS.).—The Races of Men and their Geographical Distribution. *Philadelphia*, 1848. 4to. fig. col.

× ——— 2d Edition. *London*, Bohn. 12mo.

——— The Geographical Distribution of Animals and Man. *Boston*, 1854.

PILIOLELO NO KA OLELO BERETANIA, HE.—No title. *Honolulu* (?). 8vo. pp. 40. B. (H. C.)

PIUS IX.—He Palapala apotolo a to tatou hatu hemolele loa a Pio IX, he tumutauoha ma ta oihana atua, no ta hoatata pau ana, ma te ano dogema i ta hapai pau-maele ole ia ana o ta Virigine Hanau-Atua. The dogma of the Immaculate Conception. *Honolulu*, C. M., 1856. 8vo. pp. 6. B. (H. C.)

POE (FRANCIS).—The Hawaiian Islands. [De Bow's Commercial Review. May, 1858.] *Washington*.

POLYNESIAN.—A Weekly Journal, edited by J. J. Jarves. First Series, from June 6th, 1840, to December 4th, 1841. Second Series, from May, 1844. *Honolulu*.

Bought by the Government, July, 1844, and edited by the following officials nominated by Government, J. J. Jarves, C. E. Hitchcock, Jan. 29th, 1848; C. Gordon Hopkins, Dec. 23d, 1848; Edwin O. Hall, May 14th, 1849; C. Gordon Hopkins, June 30th, 1855; Abraham Fornander, Oct., 1860.

POMARE.—Letter from Queen Pomare to Louis Phillipe, King of the French. *Honolulu*. Post 8vo. n. d.

✗ PORTLOCK (Capt. NATHANIEL).—Voyage round the world, but more particularly to the North-west coast of America, performed in 1785-88. *London*, 1789. 4to. 20 pl. See Dixon.

——— Abridged edition. *London*, 1791. 8vo. With map and portrait of Hawaiian chief.

QUATREFAGES (A. DE).—Les Polynesiens et leurs Migrations. *Paris*, 1836. 4to.

——— See Revue des Deux Mondes, Feb. 1st and 15th, 1864.

QUOY ET GAIMARD.— Zoologie du Voyage autour du monde, sur *l'Uranie* et *la Physicienne*, en 1817-20. *Paris*, 1824. 4to. et atlas de 96 pl., dont 80 coloriées.

RAE (Dr. J.).—An Essay on the great antiquity of the Hawaiian people and of their Language, and its affinities with the Sanscrit, Greek, Latin, etc., in the form of a Letter addressed to the Minister of Foreign Affairs (R. C Wyllie). *Honolulu*, 1862. Broadside. B.

READ (Rev. HOLLIS).—The Hand of God in History; or Divine Providence historically illustrated in the Extension and Establishment of Christianity. *Hartford*, 1849. 12mo.

REMY (JULES).—Recits d' un Vieux Sauvage, pour servir a l' histoire ancienne de Havaii. *Châlons-sur-Marne*, 1859. 8vo. pp. 67. B.

———— Contributions of a Venerable Savage to the ancient History of the Hawaiian Islands. Trans. by Wm. T. Brigham. *Boston*, 1868. 8vo. pp. 60. Privately printed. 200 copies. B.

———— Ka Mooolelo Hawaii. Histoire de l' Archipel Havaiien. Texte et Traduction précédés d'une Introduction sur l'etat physique, moral et politique du pays. Par [Lipalani]. *Paris* et *Leipzig*, 1862. 8vo. pp. lxxv, 254. B.

The Mooolelo alone was published in 1861.

REPORTS, annual, read before H. Majesty to the Hawaiian Legislature. *Honolulu*. Government Press, 1848. 8vo. pp. 95. (H. C.)

———— Ditto, 1850. 8vo. pp. 88. (H. C.)

———— ———— 1851. With the King's Speech. 8vo. pp. 301. (H. C.)

———— ———— 1852. Ditto. 8vo. pp. 88. (H. C.)

———— Chancery. Estate of Wm. French et al, vs. Richard Charlton and H. Skinner. *Honolulu*, 1844. 8vo. H.

———— Law. James Gray vs. Hawaiian Government. *Honolulu*, 1845. 8vo. H.

———— ———— George Pelley vs. Richard Charlton. *Honolulu*, 1844. 12mo. H.

———— ———— P. A. Brinsmade, case of libel vs. J. J. Jarves. *Honolulu*, 1846. 8vo. H.

———— ———— John Wiley, case of, seizure by a French subject. Correspondence, etc. *Honolulu*, 1844. 8vo. H.

———— ———— Ditto. Additional correspondence, 1845. H.

———— Ministerial. John Ricord, Attorney General's, 1845. *Honolulu*. 8vo. pp. 31. (H. C.)

———— ———— G. P. Judd, Minister of Interior, 1845. *Honolulu*. pp. 15. (H. C.)

———— ———— G. P. Judd, Minister of Finance, 1847. *Honolulu*. 8vo. pp. 6. (H. C.) Ditto 1854-56.

———— ———— 1846. *Honolulu*, 1846. 8vo. pp. 64. (H. C.)

REPORTS, Ministerial, 1847. H. Lea. *Honolulu.* C. E. Hitchcock, 1847. 8vo. pp. 24. (H. C.)

—————— —————— John Young, Minister of Interior, 1847. 8vo. pp. 11. (H. C.)

—————— —————— 1854-56. pp. 21, 17, 20. (H. C.)

—————— —————— Wm. Richards, Minister of Public Instruction, 1847. 8vo. pp. 12. (H. C.)

—————— —————— Ditto, 1854-55. (H. C.)

—————— —————— R. Armstrong, Minister of Public Instruction, 1854-55. pp. 18, 21. (H. C.)

—————— —————— R. C. Wyllie, Minister of Foreign Relations, 1845-47-53-54-55-56, with appendix to 1855. *Honolulu.* pp. 19, 20, 101, 95, 51, 32 and 159. (H. C.)

—————— Biennial, 1862. pp. 23.

—————— —————— R. C. Wyllie, Secretary of War, etc., 1854-55-56-62. *Honolulu.* pp. 26, 21, 277. B. (H. C.)

—————— —————— Chief Justice of the Supreme Court. First Annual Report, 1863. *Honolulu.* pp. 14. (H. C.)

—————— —————— Ditto, 1865. pp. 22. (H. C.)

—————— —————— —————— 1866. pp. 16. (H. C.)

Various Reports have been issued by Government, sometimes annually sometimes biennially, making nearly a complete series from 1845.

REPORT, Official, on the Registry of Vessels in the Hawaiian Islands. *Honolulu,* 1844. 8vo.

—————— Wyllie, R. C. Reports on the King's personal accounts, by the Commissioners of H. M. Privy Purse. *Honolulu,* 1853-55. 8vo. pp. 103, 100. (H. C.)

REPORT of the Proceedings and Evidence in the Arbitration between the King and Government of the Hawaiian Islands and Messrs. Ladd & Co., before Messrs. Stephen H. Williams and James F. B. Marshall, Arbitrators under Compact, 13th July, 1846, etc. 8vo. pp. 548, and appendix pp. 133. *Honolulu,* Oahu, Government Press, 1846. (Court Record.)

—————— Hawaiian Mission Children's Society. Annual. *Honolulu,* 1853-68. B. (H. C.)

REYNOLDS (J. N.).—Voyage of the U. S. frigate *Potomac,* during the circumnavigation of the Globe, in the years 1831-34. *New York,* 1835. 8vo.

RICHARDS (Rev. WM.).—Anahonua. Geometry for Children, translated from Holbrook. *Honolulu,* M., 1833. 16mo. pp. 64.

—————— He Mooolelo no na Holoholona wawae eha. A History of Quadrupeds. Comstock. *Lahainaluna,* 1834. 12mo. pp. 192.

RICHARDSON (J.).—Zoölogy of Capt. Beechey's Voyage, compiled from the Collections and Notes made by Capt. Beechey, the officers and Naturalist of the Expedition. *London*, Bohn, 1839. 4to. 47 pl. col.

———— Zoölogy of the Voyage of H. M. ship *Sulphur* in 1836-42. *London*, 1844. 4to. pl.

———— ———— Ichthyology. *London*, 1844. 4to. 10 pl.

RICORD (JOHN).—Award on the meaning of Lord Aberdeen's letter September 13th, 1843, in controversy with Richard Charlton claiming lands in Honolulu. *Honolulu*, 1844. 8vo. H.

ROBERTSON.—See Law Reports.

ROLAND.—See Zimmerman.

ROOKE (Dr. T. C. B.).—Remarkable Agitation of the Sea at the Sandwich Islands. [Silliman's Journal, Vol. XXXVII, p. 368.]

ROSEN.—See Steen Bille.

RUGGLES (SAMUEL).—Ninau Hoike no Kinohi. Catechism on Genesis. *Honolulu*, M., 1833. 16mo. pp. 56.

RULES AND ORDERS of the House of Representatives, etc. *Honolulu*, Government Press, 1852. 18mo.

RUSCHENBERGER (Dr. W. S. W.).—Narrative of a Voyage round the World, including an Embassy to the Sultan of Muscat, and the Kingdom of Siam. *Philadelphia* and *London*, 1838. 8vo.

———— Three Years in the Pacific. *Philadelphia*, 1854. 8vo.

Dr. Ruschenberger, surgeon of the U. S. ship *Peacock*, arrived at Honolulu Sept. 7th, 1836, and left on the 25th.

A critique on the part of the first work relating to the Hawaiian Islands, by the Rev. C. S. Stewart, appeared in the "Courier" and "Examiner" of New York, 1838, in eight letters, and a Reply in twelve letters in the "Herald" and "Sentinel" of Philadelphia.

SAINT HILAIRE (GEOFFROY).—Zoologie du Voyage autour du monde de *la Venus*, en 1838–39. *Paris*, Gide, 1855. 8vo. et atlas de 79 pl.

SAMŒDHAM.—See La Pérouse.

SANDWICH ISLAND GAZETTE and Journal of Commerce. Edited by S. D. Mackintosh. Weekly, from August 1836, to July 1839. *Honolulu*.

Established in opposition to the policy of the Government in the matter of Catholic Missionaries.

SANDWICH ISLAND MIRROR and Commercial Gazette. Monthly. Aug. 1839.

———— ———— ———— Supplement to. *Honolulu*, 1840. See Catholic Priests.

SANDWICH ISLAND MONTHLY MAGAZINE.—Monthly. Edited by A. Fornander, from January to July 1856. *Honolulu.*

SANDWICH ISLAND NEWS.—Edited by a committee of Foreign Residents. Weekly from Sept. 2, 1846, to Aug. 25th, 1847.

SANDWICH ISLANDS.— A Narrative of five youths from the, viz., Obookiah (Opukahaia), Hopoo (Hopu), Tenooe (Kanui), Honoree (Honori), and Prince Tamoree (Kamualii), now receiving an education in this country. *New York*, 1819. B. (II. C.)

This was published and sold to defray the expenses of the students.

SAUNDERS (ELIZABETH E.).— Remarks on a "Tour of Hawaii." *Salem*, 1848. 8vo. pp. 212 n. d. A.

SAXON (ISABELLE).—Five years within the Golden Gate. *London*, Chapman & Hall; *Philadelphia*, J. B. Lippincott & Co., 1868. 12mo. pp. 313.

The portion of this book relating to the Hawaiian Islands is surprisingly incorrect, even the chief town Honolulu is called Hanaruna, and where the statements can be understood at all, they are generally erroneous.

SEEMANN (BERTHOLD).—Narrative of the Voyage of H. M. ship *Herald*, during the years 1845–51; being a circumnavigation of the globe, and three cruises to the Arctic Regions in search of Sir John Franklin, under command of Henry Kellet. *London*, 1853. 2 vols. 8vo. Maps and figs.

——— German edition. *Hanover*, 1853.

Kellet arrive at Honolulu May 9th, 1847, and departed for the Arctic Ocean ten days after. Returned October 16th, 1850, and sailed for China, Nov. 3d. Seemann was the botanist of the Expedition.

SERMONS, Sixteen, in Hawaiian. *Lahainaluna*, 1836. 12mo. pp. 144. (H. C.)

SIMPSON (ALEXANDER).—The Sandwich Islands; Progress of Events since their Discovery by Capt. Cook, their occupation by Lord George Paulet, their value and importance. *London*, 1843. 8vo. Maps. (H. C.)

SIMPSON (Sir GEORGE).—Narrative of a Journey round the World during the years 1841–42, by Sir G. Simpson, Governor-in-Chief of the Hudson's Bay Company's Territories. *London*, 1847. 2 vols. 8vo. Map and portr.

Simpson arrived at the Islands Feb. 10th and left March 24th, 1842.

SKOGMAN (E.).— Voyage autour du monde sur la frégate suédoise *l'Eugéne*, en 1851–53. Observations Scientifiques, Physique,

Hydrographie, et Météorologie. *Stockholm*, 1858–61. 2 part. 4to.

SNOW (Rev. BENJAMIN G.).—Mwo sasu ma sou scmisla. Gospel of St. John in the Kusaien dialect. *Honolulu.* n. d. B. (II. C:)

SOULEYET.—See Eydoux et Souleyet.

SPARKS (JARED).—See Ledyard.

SPRENGEL (CHR.).—See La Pérouse.

SPRING (GARDNER).—Memoirs of the Rev. S. J. Mills. *New York*, 1820.

STANLEY (Earl of Derby).—On the breeding of the Sandwich Island Goose. [Proceedings of the Zoölogical Society, Vol. II., p. 41.] *London.*

STALEY (THOS. NETTLESHIP).—A Pastoral Address, by the Rt. Rev. the Bishop of Honolulu, with Notes, and a Review of the recent work of the Rev. R. Anderson, D. D., entitled, " The Hawaiian Islands." *Honolulu*, Government Press, 1865. 8vo. pp. 68. B. (H. C.)

See Alexander (W. D.).

—— —— Five Years' Church Work in the Kingdom of Hawaii. By the Bishop of Honolulu. With illustrations. London, Oxford and Cambridge, 1868. cr. 8vo. pp. 126. B.

STATUTE LAWS. See Kanawai.

—— Regulations respecting Ships, Vessels, and Harbors. *Honolulu.* n. d. 12mo.

STEEN BILLE.—Beretning om corvetten *Galathea's.* Reise omkring Jorden, 1845–47. *Copenhagen*, 1849–51. 3 vols. 8vo. Maps and pl.

—— Bericht über die Reise der corvette *Galathea* um die Welt, in den Jahren 1845–47, von Dr. W. Rosen. *Leipzig*, 1852. 2 vols. 8vo.

Steen Bille arrived at Honolulu Oct. 5th, 1846, and left Hilo, Nov. 16.

STEWART (Rev. CHAS. SAMUEL).—Private Journal of a Voyage to the Pacific Ocean, and a Residence at the Sandwich Islands, in the years 1822–25. *New York*, 1828. 12mo. pp. 406. Illus. A.

—— Second edition, with an Introduction by Rev. Wm. Ellis. *New York*, John P. Haven, 1828. (H. C.) 8vo. pp. 320.

—— Abridgement. *Dublin*, 1830.

—— Fifth edition. *Boston*, 1839. 12mo. pp. 348. A.

— 109 —

✗ STEWART (Rev. CHAS. SAMUEL).—A Visit to the South Seas, in the U. S. ship *Vincennes*, during the years of 1829–30. *New York* and *London*, 1831. 2 vols. 12mo. A.

—— Abridgement. *London*, 1832. 8vo.

    Stewart was on the Islands during this cruise, from Oct. 3d, 1829, to Nov. 24.

STRUTHERS (Rev. G.).—Memoirs of American Missionaries, with an Introductory Essay. *Glasgow*, 1834.

STURGES (Rev. ALBERT A.).—Monen pau Jon ronmau me kajira wuk ion lal en Ponope. Gospel of St. John in Ponape dialect. *Honolulu*, 1862. 8vo. pp. 39. B. (II. C.)

✗ TAYLOR (FITCH W.).—The Flag Ship, or a Voyage around the World, in the U. S. Ship *Columbia*, attended by her consort, the sloop-of-war *John Adams*, etc. *New York*, 1840. 2 vols. 12mo.

TEMPERANCE SOCIETY, THE HAWAIIAN.—Review of Mr. Wyllie's Address to the Legislature on the expediency of reducing the duties on Brandy, etc. *Honolulu*, Government Press, 1850. 8vo. pp. 16.

THIERCELIN.—Journal d'un Baleinier, Voyage en Océanie. *Paris*, 1866. 2 vols. 18mo.

✗ THOMASSY (R.).—Missions et Pêcheries, ou Politique maritime et religieuse de la France. *Paris*, 1853. 8vo.

THOMPSON (M. L. P.).—See Tinker.

THRELKELD (L. E.).—A Key to the Structure of the Languages spoken by the Aborigines in the vicinity of Hunter River, N. S. Wales; together with comparisons of Polynesian and other dialects. *Sydney*, 1850.

THURSTON (Rev. A.).—O ka hoike honua no ka Palapala Hemolele. Sacred Geography, from Worcester. *Lahainaluna*, 1834. 16mo. pp. 100. 2d edit. (H. C.)

✗ TILLEY (ARTHUR H.).—Japan, the Amoor and the Pacific, with notices of other places comprised in a Voyage of Circumnavigation in the Imperial Russian corvette *Rynda*, in 1858–60. *London* 1861.

TINKER (Rev. R.).—Sermons, with a Biographical Sketch by L. P. Thompson. *New York*, 1856.

TOWNSEND (JOHN K.).—Narrative of a Journey across the Rocky Mountains to the Columbia River, and a Visit to the Sandwich

Islands, Chili, etc.; with a Scientific Appendix. *Philadelphia*, 1839. 8vo.

TRACY (Rev. JOS.).—History of the American Board of Commissioners for Foreign Missions; compiled chiefly from the Documents of the Board. *Worcester*, 1840. 8vo.
——— 2d Edition. *Boston* and *New York*, 1842. Map.

TURNBULL (JOHN).—Voyage round the World in 1800-04, in which the Author visited the principal Islands in the Pacific Ocean, and the English settlements of Port Jackson and Norfolk Island. *London*, 1805. 3 vols. 12mo.
——— 2d Edition. *Philadelphia*, 1810.
× ——— 3d Edition, with many additions. *London*, 1813. 4to.

Turnbull arrived at the Islands, Dec. 17th, 1802, and left Jan. 21st, 1803.

× TYERMAN (Rev. DAN.) and BENNETT (GEORGE).—Journal of Voyages and Travels in the South Sea Islands, China, etc. Deputed by the London Missionary Society to visit their various stations, between the years 1821-29. Compiled from original Documents by James Montgomery. *London*, 1831. 2 vols. 8vo. Portr. and figs.
——— 2d Edition. *London*, 1840.
——— 3d Edition. *Boston*, 1832. 3 vols. 12mo.

Tyerman and Bennett arrived at the Islands in April, 1822.

UI KAMALII NO NA KULA SABATI.—Catechism. *Honolulu*, H. M. W., 1865. 8vo. Illus.

UI NO KE AKUA.—Catechism. *Honolulu*, 1862. 12mo.

UI NO KA MOOOLELO KAHIKO A KE AKUA, HE.—*Honolulu*, M., 1832. 18mo. pp. 56. B. (H. C.)

UI NO KA OLELO A KE AKUA, HE.—*Honolulu*, M., 1825. 18mo. pp. 8. Old orthography.

VAHI HOIKE KATOLIKA.—*Honolulu*, C. M., 1841. 12mo. pp. 40. (A. B. C. F. M.)

VAHI KATEKIMO, HE. — *Honolulu*, C. M., 1842. 18mo. pp. 16. (A. B. C. F. M.)
——— See Wahi.

VAILLANT.—Voyage autour du monde, exécuté pendant les années 1836-37, sur la corvette *la Bonite*, commandé par M. Vaillant, publié par ordre du Roi. *Paris*, Arthus Bertrand, 1839. 3 vols. 8vo, et album de 100 pl.

VANCOUVER (Capt. GEORGE).—A Voyage of Discovery to the North Pacific Ocean and round the World, undertaken by his Majesty's command, principally with a view to ascertain the existence of any navigable communication between the North Pacific and North Atlantic Oceans, and performed in the years 1790–95, in the *Discovery* sloop-of-war and armed tender *Chatham*, under the command of Captain George Vancouver. *London*, 1798. 3 vols. 4to, and atlas fol. 34 pl.

———— 2d Edition; corrected. *London*, 1802. 6 vols. 8vo. 19 views and maps.

———— Voyage de découvertes à l'Océan Pacifique du Nord et autour du monde, exécuté en 1790–95, par le Capitaine G. Vancouver; traduit de l'anglais par Morellet et Demeunier. *Paris*, Impr. de la Répub. an VIII. (1800). 3 vols. 4to, avec 18 figs., et atlas fol. de 16 cartes.

———— Voyage, etc., traduit par Fleury. *Paris*, an VIII. 3 vols. 4to, et atlas fol.

———— 2d Edition. *Paris*, Didot, an X. (1802). 5 vols. 8vo, et atlas fol.

Vancouver arrived at Kealakeakua, March 2d, 1792, left Niihau on the 16th, returned Feb. 12th, 1793, remaining six weeks, and again spent nine weeks at the Islands from Jan. 9th, 1794.

VIGORS (N. A.).—On a new species of Barnacle Goose, *Bernicla sandvicensis*. [Proceedings of the Zoölogical Society, Vol. I., p. 65.] *London*.

VIRGIN (C. A.).—Kongliga Svenska Fregatten *Eugenies*, Resa omkring Jorden, 1851–53, under befäl af C. A. Virgin. *Stockholm*, 1856–61. 9 part. 4to.

———— Voyage autour du monde sur la frégate suédoise *l'Eugenie*, exécuté pendant les années 1851–53. *Stockholm*, 1858–61. 2 parts. 4to.

———— German translation. *Berlin*, 1856.

———— Zoologie du Voyage autour du monde de la frégate suédoise *l'Eugenie*, en 1851–53. Annélides et Insectes. *Stockholm*, 1858. 4to.

———— N. J. Andersson. En werldsomsegling skildrad i bref, under expeditionen med Fregatten *Eugenie*, aren 1851–53. *Stockholm*, 1853–54. 3 vol.

Virgin arrived at Honolulu June 22d, 1852, left July 3d, and returned for two days in August.

VOLCANIC PHENOMENA.—See Brigham, Coan, Couthouy, Dana, Ellis, Goodrich, Green, Haldeman, Haskell, Hoffman, Jackson, Kelly, Lyman, Mann, Parker, Perrey, Stewart, etc.

VOYAGES.—Nouvelles Annales des, de la Géographie, etc., publiées sous la direction de V. A. Maltebrun.
See; 1850, t. II., p. 129;—1853, t. II., p. 318;—1856, t. III., p. 199, and t. IV., p. 15;—1859, t. III., pp. 166, 341;—1860, t. II., p. 67;—1861, t. II., p. 104;—1862, t. IV., pp. 86, 257;— 1865, t. II., p. 242, and t. III, p. 308;—etc.

——— Arranged in chronological order.

1778-79.	Cook.	1829.	Stewart, Paulding.
1786-86.	Portlock and Dixon, La-Pérouse.	1831.	Meyen, Reynolds, Wariner, Fanning.
1788.	Meares.	1834.	Bennett.
1789.	Mortimer.	1836.	Wheeler, Ruschenberger, Vaillant, Barrot.
1791.	Marchand.		
1791-93.	Colnett.	1837.	Belcher, Du Petit-Thouars, Townsend.
1792-94.	Vancouver.		
1796.	Broughton.	1838.	Lœwenstern, Taylor, Laplace.
1802.	Turnbull.		
1803.	Cleveland.	1840.	Wilkes, Olmstead, Dana, Pickering.
1804.	Krusenstern, Lisianski, Langsdorff.	1842.	Simpson.
1806.	Mariner.	1844.	Hines.
1809.	Campbell, Delano.	1846.	Walpole, Steen Bille.
1815-17.	Corney.	1847.	Kellett, Seeman.
1816.	Kotzebue, Chamisso, Choris.	1848.	Wise, Wood (W. M.), Colton.
1819.	Freycinet, Arago.	1849.	Hill, Perkins.
1822.	Mathison, Tyerman and Bennet.	1852.	Virgin, Andersson.
		1853.	Bates, Gerstaecker.
1824.	Kotzebue.	1854.	Febvrier Despointes.
1825.	Byron, Morrell.	1855.	Egerstrœm.
1826.	Beechey.	1859.	Tilley, Aylmer.
1828.	Duhaut-Cilley, Lafond de Lurcy.	1864-65.	Brigham, Mann.

WAHI MAU NIELE NO KA PALAPALA HONUA.—Geographical Question Book. 2d Edition. *Lahainaluna*, 1837. 12mo. pp. 44. (A. B. C. F. M.)

WAHI MOOOLELO, HE, no ta hoomainoino ia ana o ta poe Kiritiano ma te aupuni Anamita, mai ta hoolaha ana o ta evanelio malaila a hiti i teia va. *Hor olulu*, C. M., 1857. 8vo. pp. 20. B. (H. C.)

——— See Vahi.

WALCKENAER.—Le Monde maritime ou tableau géographique et historique de l'Archipel de l'Orient, etc. 4 vol. *Paris*, Breton.

× WALPOLE (F.).—Four years in H. M. ship *Collingwood*. London, 1849. 2 vols. 8vo.

——— Four years in the Pacific from 1844 to 1848, with Sports and Adventures among the Islands. *London*, 1850. 2 vols. 8vo. Illus.

Walpole arrived Aug. 6th, and left Sept 8th, 1846.

× WARRINER (FR.).—Journal of a cruise in the U. S. frigate *Potomac*. round the world, in 1831–34. *New York*, 1835. 12mo.

At the Islands in 1832.

WASHBURN (I., Jun.).—The Sandwich Islands. Speech in the U. S. House of Representatives, Jan. 4th, 1854. *Washington*. 8vo, pp. 7. (H. C.)

WEBBER (JAS.).—Views in the South Seas, from drawings by the late James Webber, from the year 1775 to 1780. *London*, Boydell, 1808. Fol. 16 pl. col.

WHEELER (DANIEL).—Extracts from the Letters and Journals of D. Wheeler, now engaged in a Religious Visit to some of the Islands of the Pacific Ocean, Van Diemen's Land and New South Wales. *London*, 1839. 8vo.
——— 2d Edition. *Philadelphia*, 1840. 8vo.
——— Abridgement. *Philadelphia*, 1859.

Wheeler arrived at the Hawaiian Islands Dec. 26th, 1835, and left June 16th, 1836.

WHITNEY (Rev. SAMUEL).—He Hoike Honua. From Woodbridge's Geography. *Honolulu*, M., 1836. 12mo. pp. 203.
——— 2d Edition, 1845. 62 woodcuts. B. (H. C.)
——— He mau Haawina no ka Palapala Hemolele. Bible Class Book. *Lahainaluna*, 1839. 2 vols. 12mo. pp. 36, 40.
——— Hoike uhane. Child's Book on the Soul; trans. from Gallaudet. *Honolulu*, M., 1840. 18mo. pp. 66. Vol. I. (H. C.)
——— and RICHARDS.—Hoike Honua. Geography. *Honolulu*, M., 1832. 12mo. pp. 40.

× WILKES (CHARLES).—Narrative of the United States Exploring Expedition, executed in the years 1838 to 1842, under the command of Charles Wilkes, U. S. N. *Philadelphia*, 1845. 5 vols. 4to. Maps and illus.
——— 2d Edition, 1849. 5 vols. 8vo. Illus.
——— 3d Edition. *New York*, 1852. 5 vols. 8vo. Maps, 111 pl. on steel and 300 woodcuts.

WILKES (CHARLES).—4th Edition. *New York*, 1856. 5 vols. Large 8vo. 14 maps, 64 pl., 47 vignettes on steel, and 250 woodcuts.

⸺ Abridgement. *London*, 1845. 8vo.

⸺ Voyage round the World, embracing the principal events of the Narrative of the United States Exploring Expedition. *New York*, 1851. 8vo. 170 illus.

⸺ Lights and Shadows of a Sailor's Life, being a Narrative of the United States Exploring Expedition. *Boston*, 1847.

Wilkes arrived at the Islands Sept. 24th, 1840.

⸺ Meteorology of the United States Exploring Expedition. Journal of Meteorological Observations. *Philadelphia*, 1851. 4to. 25 woodcuts. Map and 24 pl.

WILLIAMS (JOHN).—Narrative of Missionary Enterprises in the South Sea Islands, with Remarks on the Natural History of the Islands, Origin, Languages, Traditions and Usages of the Inhabitants. *London*, 1837. 8vo. Map and illus.

⸺ 1st American Edition. *New York*, D. Appleton & Co., 1837. 8vo. pp. 525. B.

WILTBERGER (C.).—Temperance Map. *Lahainaluna*, 1843. 18mo. pp. 16. B. (H. C.)

WISE.—Los Gringos; or, an Inside View of Mexico and California, with Wanderings in Peru, Chili and Polynesia. *New York* and *London*, 1849.

⸺ 2d Edition. *New York*, 1857. 12mo.

At the Islands in September, 1848.

WIZARD OF THE NORTH.—A series of Letters published in the Aberdeen "Herald."

WOOD (Rev. GEO. W.).—Special Report on Interference in Foreign Missions presented to the A. B. C. F. M., Sept., 1866. *Boston*, 1866. 8vo. pp. 12. (H. C.)

WOOD (Dr. R. W.).—Sandwich Islands: Climate, Population, Government, Productions, Commerce, Reciprocity Treaty with the United States. [De Bow's Commercial Review, etc., March, 1857.] *Washington*.

WOOD (Dr. W. M.).—Wandering Sketches of People and Things in South America, Polynesia, California, and other places visited during a cruise in the U. S. ships *Levant, Portsmouth* and *Savannah*. *Philadelphia*, 1849. 8vo.

WYLLIE (ROBERT CRICHTON).—Notes on the Shipping, Trade, Agriculture, Climate, Diseases, Religious Institutions, Civil and Social Condition, Mercantile and Financial Policy of the Sandwich or Hawaiian Islands, viewed in relation to other Groups of Islands, and to the natural and acquired advantages of the Sandwich or Hawaiian Islands. *Honolulu*, 1845. 8vo.

See "Friend," May, 1845, etc., and "Colonial Magazine," London, 1846.

―――― Address to the House of Representatives of the Hawaiian Kingdom by Robert Crichton Wyllie, Minister of Foreign Relations. *Honolulu*, 1850. 8vo. pp. 41. See Temperance Society.

―――― See Correspondence; and Reports.

ZIMMERMAN (HEINRICH).—Reise um die Welt mit Capit. Cook *Gottingen*, 1781. 8vo.

―――― Dernier Voyage du Capt. Cook autour du monde, ou se trouve les circonstances de sa mort, par H. Zimmerman, témoin oculaire, traduit etc. par Roland. *Berne*, 1782. 8vo.

ZOOLOGY.—See Bennett, Brandt, Cassin, Chamisso, Dana, Eschscholtz, Eydoux et Souleyet, St. Hilaire, Gould, Gray, Haldeman, Hinds, Kittlitz, Laurent, Peale, Quoy et Gaimard, Richardson, Virgin.

HE MELE LAHUI HAWAII.

KE MELE A ME NA HUAMELE,

HAKUIA E

MRS. LILIA K. DOMINIS.

Ka Ma-ku-a Ma-na Loa, Ma-li-u mai ia

ma-kou E ha-li-u a-ku nei Me ka na-au ha-a-

haa. E mau ka ma-lu--hia, O nei Pae Ai-

na, Mai Ha-wai-i a Nii - hau Ma-la-lo o kou-ma-

lu E mau ka Ea o ka Ai-na, Ma kou po-no

mau a ma-kou ma-na nui, E o-la, e o-la ka Mo-i.

>Malalo *o* kou aloha nui,
>Na' Lii o ke Aupuni,
>Me na Makaainana,
>Ka lehulehu no a pau;
>Kiai mai ia lakou
>Me ke aloha ahonui;
>E ola no makou
>I kou mana mau.
>*Hooho.*—E mau ke ea o ka aina
>   A pela aku.

ARTICLES OF ORGANIZATION

OF THE

HAWAIIAN CLUB.

I. The name of this Association shall be the HAWAIIAN CLUB.

II. Its object shall be to promote social intercourse among the friends of Hawaii, resident in or visiting Boston and vicinity, and to advance the interests of the United States at the Hawaiian Islands, and the welfare of the Hawaiian nation, by collecting and diffusing information bearing thereupon, and by all other honorable means.

III. The members of the Club shall be those persons in attendance upon the meeting at which the Club shall be organized, who shall sign these Articles, with such others as may at any properly called meeting thereafter be elected by ballot. Two ballots in opposition to any one nominated shall defeat his election. Honorary members may be elected in the same manner, and under the same restriction.

IV. The officers of the Club shall be a President, a Vice-President, a Secretary, who shall act as Treasurer, and two Directors, who together shall constitute an Executive Committee, and who shall manage the affairs of the Club, and direct about the collection and disbursement of funds, and the publication of documents. They shall hold office for one year, and until their successors shall have been appointed.

V. The annual meeting of the Club shall be held on the third Wednesday of January of each year, at which meeting the officers for the ensuing year shall be chosen by ballot. There shall be a regular meeting of the Club on the third Wednesday of each month. Special meetings may be called by the President. Five shall constitute a quorum.

VI. The expenses of the Club for stationery, publications, etc., shall be met by voluntary contributions.

VII. These Articles can be amended at any duly called meeting.

HAWAIIAN CLUB.

OFFICERS FOR 1868.

President, JAMES HUNNEWELL.
Vice President, JAMES F. B. MARSHALL.
Secretary and Treasurer, EDWARD P. BOND.
Directors, CHARLES BREWER, BENJAMIN PITMAN.

Editing Committee, { WILLIAM T. BRIGHAM, JAMES F. HUNNEWELL, SANFORD B. DOLE.

Original Members, January 19, 1868.

Edward P. Bond,
George Brayton,
Charles Brewer,
Edward M. Brewer,
G. D. Gilman,
James Hunnewell,
Peter C. Jones,
James N. Lindsey,
Charles H. Lunt,
David B. Lyman,
James F. B. Marshall,
Benjamin Pitman,
Wm. Franklin Snow,
David M. Weston,
Hiram B. White.

William Andrews,
William N. Armstrong,
Samuel C. Armstrong,
William P. Avis,
Stephen Bailey,
Daniel C. Bigelow,
William T. Brigham,
Wesley Burnham,
Henry A. P. Carter,
Titus M. Coan,
George S. Cushing,
Sanford B. Dole,
James R. Dow,
Justin Emerson,
Nathaniel B. Emerson,
Warren Goodale,
James D. Hague,
S. Holmes,
James F. Hunnewell,
John Q. A. Johnson,
Henry M. Lyman,
Horace Mann,
Charles Pickering,
William Reynolds,
Augustus Russ,
John A. Sleeper,
Edwin Stevens,
John W. Sullivan,
James B. Williams,
Robert W. Wood.

www.ingramcontent.com/pod-product-compliance
Lightning Source LLC
Chambersburg PA
CBHW031348160426
43196CB00007B/776